Cat and Bird

Cat and Bird

a memoir by Kyoko Mori

Belt Publishing

Printed in the United States of America
First edition
1 2 3 4 5 6 7 8 9

ISBN: 978-1-953368-69-0

Belt Publishing
13443 Detroit Avenue, Lakewood, OH 44107
www.beltpublishing.com

Cover art and book design by David Wilson

This is a work of nonfiction. The names of some characters have been changed to protect their privacy.

In memory of Katherine Russell Rich, an intrepid traveler who was at home anywhere and everywhere—

Table of Contents

Prologue

The stories I tell are the spokes of a wheel in perpetual motion. Their sources are as constant and elusive as birds migrating across the hemispheres. Whenever I sit down at my desk, alone but together with my cats, the act of writing becomes a ceremony of stillness. Even though Dorian, Oscar, Ernest, and Algernon are no longer with me, writing about them with Miles and Jackson by my side, I am suspended in a timeless place where I can hold on to them and let them go at once and for always. Remembering and forgetting are the two hands of the clock moving forward and backward: they are separate, interchangeable, and indispensable to one another. Capturing the truth and releasing it back into the world is the point of arranging and rearranging the words. As birds gather and scatter outside our window, I have to believe that from our shelter on the ground, I can help keep their wings beating.

Chapter One

The Chimney Swift

All migratory birds are affected by climate change, but the more immediate threat to swifts in North America is the difficulty of finding a place to sleep during their fall migration. The old trees in whose hollows they once rested as they traveled south in enormous flocks are long gone. The first houses with chimneys that replaced the forests have been torn down as well. New houses built in their place have chimneys with ceramic interiors too slippery for the birds' feet, which leaves old buildings, like my brownstone in the nation's capital, as their only roosting sites. However, because their fall migration overlaps with the start of winter heating season, many buildings have elected to cover their chimneys with screens to keep the birds out. If a boiler is turned on while upwards of five hundred birds are roosting in the chimney above it, the carbon monoxide will cause them to die and fall to the bottom, a disaster even for people who don't care about wildlife.

Since the swifts' migration through our region is over by the last week of October, it's easy to monitor the sky nightly and turn on the boiler after the birds are gone. Only a few days in October are noticeably cold in Washington, DC, and even on those days, the temperature is not so low that an extra sweater can't keep warm every human in the building. But every year, the same few people in my building complained about being cold and asked to have the chimney covered and the heat turned on as early as October 1. They argued that humans shouldn't have to "sacrifice for the birds," even after being informed that swifts were known to circle newly covered chimneys, persistently trying to get in and exhausting themselves in the process. Migratory birds don't have a lot of energy to waste, and they often take years to alter their route by even a few miles, so if we covered our chimney, the swifts that relied on it would keep coming back anyway. Some would die in the cold and the dark while looking for another resting spot at the last minute.

I couldn't understand how anyone could value the smallest detail of their own comfort over the life and death of a whole flock of birds, but the few neighbors who got hysterical every time the temperature dropped below forty-five degrees while the building's radiators remained "stone cold" were beyond my ability to educate about wildlife, climate change, or ecological conscientiousness. One of them claimed that when she bought her apartment, she was not intending to live in a wildlife preserve.

The easiest way for me to ensure that our chimney stayed open and the boiler got turned on only after the birds were gone (and turned off before they came back—though in smaller numbers—in late April or early May) was to be in charge of making and carrying out the building's heating policy. So I volunteered to be on our co-op's board of directors and stayed on as president to protect the swifts— and eventually, to protect the majority of residents who were reasonable people—from the same few who only cared about themselves.

On the concrete floor of the boiler room, the chimney swift resembled a black fan knocked out of a flamenco dancer's hand. About five inches long from head to tail, the bird lay flat on its chest, its curved wings folded, crossed over the tail feathers.

In the sky, a swift's wings can span twelve inches as the bird soars and glides while catching and holding two hundred midges or mosquitoes in its mouth. Chimney swifts spend the whole day in the air and rest at night by clinging vertically to rough surfaces, such as the bricks inside of chimneys. In that position, their hooked feet can support their weight for hours, but if a swift falls from its roost, as this one must have, it is unable to stand upright and hop.

My building was built in 1923, and the bottom of the chimney is inside the locked boiler room. A bird trapped there would have weakened and died unnoticed, but I was in the basement that spring morning with Roosevelt, our cheerful and capable pest control guy, who, in the six years I'd been the co-op's board president, had dealt with everything from deer mice to bedbugs. Roosevelt is over six feet tall, and he can single-handedly take down wasps' nests and shove dishwashers out of the way to check for roaches and mouse droppings. Always easygoing and talkative, that morning, he suddenly went silent, and I thought a bird trapped indoors might be new for him because it was something to be saved, not exterminated.

The swift fluttered up to the window, slid down, and fell back to the floor, where it sat rocking slightly on its chest. I asked Roosevelt to wait and ran up to my apartment to get a paper bag. When I returned, he and the bird were exactly where I'd left them. I knelt on the floor and closed my fingers around the swift's back, pinning its wings shut. It didn't resist being picked up. But the moment I dropped it into the bag and closed my fist around the top, it began to move and flap. Through two double-locked metal doors, up the stairs, and along the side of the building to the backyard, the bird's wings were beating like firecrackers inside the bag.

Cat and Bird

It was the last week of May. I knew by then the chimney swifts had left their wintering grounds in the upper Amazon basin of Peru, Chile, and Brazil to disperse through their breeding range, which stretches from northern Florida to southern Canada. Any swift who was here in the spring would be at least one year old. The bird I was about to release had already migrated to the Amazon and back—ten thousand miles at least. Swifts travel north in small flocks, their numbers dwindling as pairs break away to build their nests in old chimneys along the way. The bird in my hand might spend the summer raising its young in our chimney on the other side of my bedroom wall.

I tipped the bag and slid the swift onto a picnic table. In the morning light, its feathers looked sooty brown. The swift pushed itself up off the table and ascended the clearing in ever-widening circles. I counted the spirals—three, four, five—until the bird rose over the treetops, where every evening for the last few weeks, a dozen swifts had appeared at dusk to circle, forage, and dive into our chimney.

Back in the boiler room, Roosevelt was securing packets of bait in the mouse and roach traps. I thanked him and returned to my apartment, where my two cats, Miles and Jackson, were sleeping on the bed adjacent to the chimney flue. They lay belly to belly, their legs tangled together, their heads touching. They had been keeping me company since 2010, when Ernest and Algernon, the pair of Siamese cats who had moved with me from Boston to Washington in 2005, died within months of each other. Miles arrived first, and then Jackson six months later. Now Miles was three, Jackson two and a half.

I picked Jackson up and held him aloft over my head, one hand under his chest, the other under his hips, supporting and stretching his dark brown body into a flying posture with his legs extended forward and backward. I spun around slowly, moving him in the pattern of a swift's flight, dipping down, tilting sideways, and rising up again. Both of my cats are famous, or infamous, for being docile. Jackson remained relaxed, airborne, while Miles opened his eyes, rounded his back, and settled to sleep once more, camouflaged by the bedcovers that matched his light gray coloring. I lowered Jackson but held on to him while I flopped down on the bed next to Miles, thinking of the swift migrating through a sky full of danger. I pressed Jackson to my chest and buried my face in Miles's fur, then closed my eyes.

"A good day already," I told them. "I saved a bird."

After Roosevelt and I found the fallen swift, I checked the boiler room whenever it rained hard overnight and often came across one or two birds. They fluttered around the piles of cleaning and gardening supplies, then clung to the wall to rest, dark and immobile like an old-fashioned door knocker, so it was easy to pluck them off, put them in a bag, take them outside, and set them free. Like most otherwise gregarious birds, swifts become territorial during their mating season. No matter how large the chimney, there is only one nest. The breeding male and female may tolerate a few birds that didn't find mates for the season, but no other pair is allowed in the flue. So by early June, the few swifts that went into our chimney every night were the ones who'd settled in there for the summer, and I must have been catching and releasing the same birds over and over. I left a stack of paper bags, a flashlight, and a stepladder next to the boiler.

I had been tracking swift migration for several years, noting the first flock's arrival and anticipating the pair that would nest in our building. In early summer, when the eggs hatched, the parents would start diving in and out of the chimney all day long to feed their nestlings. By the time the young emerged, they were indistinguishable from their parents and could fly and feed in midair. A compact flock of eight or nine birds foraged in the sky and dove into the chimney at dusk, but they were scarcely noticeable unless you were looking for them.

Then one evening in late August, the first flock of migrating swifts came through, thirty or forty birds wheeling around, filling the sky with loud chattering and clicking calls. The birds from our chimney would have been gone by then, roosting with another flock farther south. Just how many nights each bird roosts in the same chimney on its way south is unknown, but the flocks migrate in waves. We'd get the largest wave around the first week of October, and then the birds would thin out to just ten or twenty every night until one evening in late October, the sky would be suddenly empty of swifts.

Swift-viewing from the driveway with snacks and glasses of wine was the default social event among the dozen neighbors who were my close friends. At the migration's peak, we could count over five hundred birds circling our chimney. Several of them would hover near the chimney's opening, maneuvering around each other in such a way that you could hear their wings flapping over their loud calls while hundreds more swirled above. You could see them dive in one at a time, like smoke whirling back into the flue. In the last few minutes before the sky completely darkened, they would drop into the chimney so fast you could only count them in estimated clusters of ten. And just when you thought they were done for the night, two or three birds would appear out of nowhere, zip around the sky a few times, and finally turn in. My friends and I, too, would gather our glasses and plates and head inside.

If no one was around, I watched from inside my apartment, through the windows' original century-old cylinder glass that had striations like ripples on a quiet pond. The angle wasn't right to observe the birds' final dive into the chimney—for that, I would have had to open one of my living room windows, remove the pots of flowers I'd placed on the ledge, and lean out as far as I could without falling—but with the windows closed for safety, I could view the swifts gathering and circling in preparation, wheeling in and out of my field of vision. After years of trying to keep the cats off the dining table, I'd hop up there myself to sit with my face pressed to the windowpane. Eventually, Miles and Jackson ended up on my lap, on my shoulder, or next to me. Because the swifts were high up in the air, the cats couldn't see them, so they usually fell asleep.

Our three-story building with twenty-seven apartments has just one chimney that serves the boiler system. My apartment is on the top floor, in the column adjacent to the flue, so of all the residents, my cats and I sleep closest to the roosting swifts. The chimney rises about twelve feet above the roof, and there is a three-foot crawl space between the roof and my ceiling. If the swifts filled up all of that space, some of them would have to cling to the bricks beside my bed. I don't know how far down the birds had to go to roost for the night, but even in their sleep, swifts were said to continue their chatter. Some nights, I would stand on my bed and put my ear to the wall. But I never heard anything. I'd hold my cats aloft and press their ears to the wall as well, hoping their keener sense of hearing might detect a faint bird sound, but they'd look down at me in total incomprehension.

Cat and Bird

Chimney swifts were once called North American swifts. They roosted in tree hollows across the Eastern United States until the early settlers cleared acres of forests to build houses, at which point the birds started using the bricks inside chimneys. Swifts eat flying insects in the air, so unlike birds that can be fed on seeds, grains, or mealworms from a dish, adult swifts cannot be held in captivity for research. Theirs is a story of adaptation, of wildlife managing to live in close quarters with humans, but only a few ornithologists with special mirrors and cameras have been able to observe their nesting and roosting habits inside chimneys. Swifts practically sleep inside our houses, and yet we humans know so little about them. Even their evolutionary origin is a mystery.

Swifts and hummingbirds, who have a common ancestor, migrate on similar schedules. Every October, dusk falls on the dwindling flocks of swifts as I watch the last hummingbird of the season make a stop at the sugar feeder in my flowerpot. A female, fattened up for her nonstop flight over the Gulf of Mexico, hovers among the purple salvias like a tropical fish swimming through air. Ruby-throated hummingbirds, the species that visits my windows, do not form pairs or flocks; they are solitary even during migration.

From one prehistoric bird descended soot-colored swifts who congregate in the hundreds, and iridescent hummingbirds who travel alone to locations unknown to them. Neither can hop to cover even a short distance on the ground. What they share is the ability—and also the need—to keep moving in midair.

Chapter Two

Escaped Parakeet

In Kobe, Japan, where I grew up in the 1960s, my mother scattered seeds and breadcrumbs on our balcony for the house sparrows that congregated in noisy, voracious flocks. In the bedtime stories she told me, animals returned to the people who had rescued them from hunters' traps and warned them about an approaching forest fire or helped them find buried treasure. Unlike the friends I made as an adult in America, who were raised on farms or in small towns in the Midwest, I had been encouraged by my mother to be softhearted about wildlife.

The first bird that ever fell in my path was a house sparrow. I came across it on a sidewalk near the coffee shop where I waitressed in secret the summer I was fifteen. My father and stepmother would have been horrified: girls from well-to-do families did not dress up in a maid's uniform and serve sandwiches to strangers. I received a monthly allowance from my father; in ten years, I was expected to have a husband who provided the same. But I wanted money of my own, even if it was a pittance. The coffee shop was in a neighborhood of offices near a commuter train station a couple of miles away from our house. My stepmother believed I was taking swimming lessons at a health club with some friends.

The sparrow landed at my feet and stayed there, hunched over with his wings dragging on the hot pavement. He didn't fly away when I crouched over him. I picked him up as easily as I would a tennis ball. There was no cut or blood anywhere on his body. Though his eyes were closed, his heart was beating. A group of young women in summer dresses and white sandals came walking in my direction, chatting and laughing.

Cat and Bird

I stood up, opened my tote bag, and tucked the sparrow in between my swimsuit and the towel I'd packed as evidence of my swimming lessons; then, in a housewares store down the street, I bought a pale blue colander and a tiny ceramic sake cup. The coffee shop was just a few doors away, on the ground floor of a row house. The owner, a divorced woman my stepmother's age, lived on the second floor; the third floor had a small bathroom where I changed into my uniform, a white apron over a purple polyester dress.

Inside the bathroom, I opened the tote bag and half-expected the sparrow to be dead, but his chest was still moving. I lifted him out and positioned him, feet first, on the tiled floor of the shower stall. He slumped forward with his eyes closed, but he didn't fall over. He remained right side up with his feet folded underneath him. I filled the sake cup with water and placed it next to him. If he stood up, he'd be able to drink from it. Even if he didn't, this was a better place to die than on the sidewalk, where a passerby could step on him. I covered the sparrow with the pale blue colander—the only item in the store that remotely resembled a birdcage—and hoped the color would remind him of the sky.

The coffee shop was the size of a living room and had six small tables. Customers came in twos and threes: office workers, college students, and workmen from nearby buildings under renovation. I was the only lunch waitress; the cook, a quiet middle-aged man, stood behind the counter, making sandwiches and plating salads.

The owner, whose orangey-red lipstick was just like my stepmother's, usually came down from her apartment to talk to the cook, take inventory of her supplies, and make a few phone calls, but she was gone that afternoon. Had she been home, she might have heard the raspy *tchup-tchup-tchup* vibrating from the floor above her.

Three hours later, after my shift was over, I was halfway up the stairs to the third floor when I heard a loud bird call. I sprinted the rest of the way. I peered through the colander in the shower stall and saw the bird hopping back and forth and pecking at the tiled floor. His beak's downward motion barely interrupted his scolding vocalization. He must have been stunned when I had first found him—maybe he flew into a window or was suffering from heatstroke. No matter—his condition had been temporary.

The only window in the bathroom was behind the toilet, and it was higher than I was tall. I climbed on the tank and pushed up the lower frame. The window opened only a few inches, but at least there wasn't a screen. I went back to the shower stall and lifted the colander. The sparrow immediately hopped out and flew around the room, unafraid and unhurt. His raspy call was even louder now. No longer the sick bird in my palm, he was just an ordinary sparrow, like the hundreds that would peck at my mother's bread crumbs before she killed herself and they stopped coming. It would have been difficult to catch him and put him outside, but soon enough, he figured it out on his own. He flew first to the top of the toilet tank and then to the window ledge, pausing only a moment before slipping through the small opening and disappearing from view.

I closed the window and cleaned the tiled floor, where the sparrow had knocked over the sake cup and left his white droppings. Then I changed into my street clothes and headed to the city pool, where I swam a few laps so my hair and my swimsuit would smell convincingly of chlorine.

Back home in my bedroom, I hid the sake cup and the blue colander in my closet. They sat there for years. Though I couldn't have explained why, it didn't seem right to throw them away. They were among the things I left behind when I moved to America at the age of twenty and made my own escape through a window's narrow opening to be like any other girl who once had a mother to love her.

After I had taken a few birds to the wildlife sanctuary in Green Bay, Wisconsin, where I was living and teaching in my thirties, I wanted to learn what to do beyond lifting the poor things off the ground, putting them in a cardboard box, and driving them across town. So I signed up to be trained as a bird rehabilitator.

Concerned citizens brought in baby birds that had been knocked out of their nests by storms, tree trimmers, or predators, and I became one of the volunteers on call who took the birds home, cared for them, and then released them back into the wild. The care of migratory birds is strictly regulated by the US Fish and Wildlife Service. It's illegal to keep wildlife at home, even with the good intention of nursing a wounded animal back to health, but I was licensed through the training program at the sanctuary.

At first, the nestlings were unable to stand, let alone fly. They were just a bundle of bones inside dull gray skin. Even healthy birds looked deformed at two or three days old, and it was difficult to distinguish between species except by size. Once I brought them home, they had to be placed in a cup-shaped container—usually a berry box lined with tissue—with their feet tucked underneath them so their legs would develop properly. Most of them would lift their heads, stretch their necks, open their mouths, and clamor for food when I tapped the side of the berry box to imitate the sound of their parents' feet landing on the nest. They grew fast, sprouting pinfeathers and fattening by the day. I'd put the simulated nest inside a plastic laundry basket, topped with another basket turned upside down. Robins, house finches, cedar waxwings, chipping sparrows, Eastern kingbirds—each species was kept together in its provisional nest inside a separate basket. The sanctuary placed several birds of the same species with each volunteer, so the nestlings would grow up recognizing others of their kind. To survive in the wild, birds must learn where their species congregates to feed, roost, migrate, and mate. As the proverb says, birds of a feather flock together. Solitary birds, like ruby-throated hummingbirds, are rare.

When it was fourteen to twenty days old, a nestling would stand up in the berry box for the first time and climb onto its edge. There, it would lean first on one leg and then on the other to open and preen its wings before hopping down to explore the laundry basket's paper-lined floor. Birds that left the nest never returned to sit in it; I'd place twigs and small branches inside the baskets so they could practice perching and spreading their wings. A few times a day, I'd take them out and let them fly around the room, then pry them off the woven tapestry where they'd land and cling.

In order to keep them from becoming too tame, no one else was allowed to handle the birds once they were in my care. The nestlings were not for show-and-tell. The work I did at home, alone in a quiet room, allowed them to be wild and safe only with me. Bird rehabilitators provided a controlled environment where more birds survived than they would have with parents who couldn't nourish them, especially if predators were present. Only 10 percent of the nestlings born every summer live long enough to become adults. Most songbirds lay four to six eggs two or three times every season to make up for the ones that are inevitably lost.

Once the birds in my care could fly, I'd transfer them to the walk-in cage in my backyard, where they'd practice foraging. Beautiful birds, like cedar waxwings and Eastern kingbirds, I felt lucky to see up close, and the more common birds, like robins and finches, I enjoyed for their distinct personalities. Some robins were bent on trusting me too much, hopping right behind me as I walked around the cage. I had to break them of this habit by not feeding them every time they came to me. Others would screech and back into a corner, only to open their beaks, flutter their wings, and beg to be fed. Apparently, a fear of intimacy and the tendency to project mixed messages were not the sole province of humans.

I was like the escaped parakeet a friend once saw flying in a flock of starlings. I left Japan in 1977 to attend college in Illinois and graduate school in Milwaukee before settling in Green Bay to teach writing and literature at a small Catholic college. I married a man who had grown up a few miles away from where we lived, but because I'm Japanese, most people assumed I was just visiting. Strangers would stop me in the grocery store and at the gas station and ask me where I was from. They'd compliment me on my ability to speak English and wonder why I was living so far from home. Many of them had grandparents who had immigrated from Sweden, Holland, Norway, Poland, Germany, or Ireland, and yet they were surprised to hear I had become an American citizen. They always referred to Japan as "your country." I stopped telling them that I was a writer and an English professor, because that revelation inexorably led to questions like, "You mean, *you* teach English to Americans?" and, "Wow, it must have taken a long time for you to write stories in a foreign language," or, "Do you translate every word in your head, or do you first write it in Japanese?"

The wildlife rehabilitators I met at the sanctuary didn't care where I was from. They wanted to know how many cedar waxwings the intake volunteer had given me and if I knew the difference between a song sparrow, a white-throated sparrow, and a chipping sparrow. They showed me the popular birdwatching spots around town and invited me to meetings of the Audubon Society. Getting to know the birds—and the people devoted to their welfare—gave me at least a small community of like-minded friends.

Although my main motive was my personal interest in birds, volunteering at the wildlife sanctuary was more than a hobby. Each rehabilitator had to keep meticulous records for the sanctuary's licensing requirements and for educating the public. Whenever someone called to ask about the bird they'd brought in, we gave them a progress report and then talked about what they could do to help protect songbirds—refraining from using pesticides on their lawn, suspending tree work and construction projects until after the height of the bird breeding season, and planting native grasses and flowers in their yard. Since most of the birds we rescued belonged to abundant rather than threatened species, we had a greater impact on the community by teaching ecological awareness than by increasing the number of rare birds that survived.

The formula for feeding the nestlings, along with other instructions, came from the sanctuary's rehab manual, a hefty black binder of mimeographed sheets compiled by generations of volunteer rehabilitators going back to the 1960s. The birds that clamored for food learned to associate the beak-like shape of the feeding syringe—and through it, me—with their parents.

Cat and Bird

Feeding a reluctant bird, on the other hand, required dexterity, timing, and concentration, a combination that came easily to me, which was surprising since no one would have described me as necessarily having such skills. I broke knickknacks while cleaning the house and couldn't hang pictures on the wall without banging my fingers with a hammer. I was flummoxed by tools, gadgets, and a host of inanimate objects both large and small, but an animal in need was a different story altogether. The moment I was alone with my charge, all the distractions fell away, leaving the two of us inside a magic circle, where every detail was magnified and I could perform any complicated task as if I was born knowing how to do it. If I ever had a "calling," this was it.

In my kitchen blender, I'd mix bird vitamins with high-protein cat food soaked in water, grapes, or blueberries, then suction the soupy formula into a needle-less syringe. For the first two weeks, the birds would sit in the nest and sleep with their necks slumped forward, heads down, and I'd feed them from sunrise to sundown. My summer break from teaching coincided perfectly with bird breeding season, so I could stay home all day to care for them and work on my writing. Every fifteen minutes, I'd run from my ersatz office in the basement to the bird nursery on the second floor to feed them.

Over the course of a few weeks, the birds would grow, and the coloring of their feathers and the shape of their beaks would become more pronounced. Chipping sparrows revealed their eye stripes, though they were still very faint. Finches with conical beaks and streaked breasts emerged from their dull and mottled juvenile plumage. By the time the birds left their berry-box nests and started flying around the room, they looked distinctively like their particular species; the nestlings had become fledglings, and they were ready to move on to the outdoor cage, where they'd line up on a branch I'd rigged for them, flutter their wings, and open their mouths. This is where we would practice their survival skills. I fed them just enough to keep them strong but left them hungry so they'd forage for the seeds, fruits, grains, and worms I'd left for them to discover. The birds that continued to come to me were easier to monitor than those that hid. Still, it's not natural for a bird to grow up perceiving a human to be nurturing or benign. Some rehabilitators who raised birds that were likely to be harmed by people—such as cranes, owls, eagles, and wild turkeys—wore disguises or used hand puppets.

The small songbirds in my care, however, had no value as food, illegal pets, or trophies, so they had less to fear from humans. The most important lesson a house finch needed to learn was how to feed itself from the ubiquitous cylindrical birdseed feeders in our town's backyards. I trained them by using a syringe of food to lure them to the feeder that I'd hung inside the cage, then getting them to perch on its metal rungs and tempting them to peck at the seed ports by smearing the formula there. There were always six or seven finches at any one time in the outdoor cage, and in each group, one finch would figure out the bird feeder first, and the others would follow suit. They learned through imitation, just as they would have if their parents had flown with them for a week or two, showing them possible food sources and roosting sites.

Soon, I'd stop going to the backyard with the formula, and I would watch the birds through binoculars until they were all eating from the feeder and the flock was ready to be released. Most of the birds I cared for were common in residential gardens, so I could just open the cage and let them go. Robins, house finches, waxwings, chipping sparrows, and mourning doves would disperse themselves into flocks already summering in our neighborhood. Though I released more than thirty finches every summer, none of them came back to beg food from me; for all I knew, they were eating from my own cylindrical feeder right outside my kitchen window. In the wild, birds don't stay with their parents or siblings once they know how to feed themselves. First-year birds join and circulate within the larger flock, leaving the parents free to lay their next clutch of eggs. They congregate with their own kind, not with their original family.

The Eastern kingbird was an exception. The one in my care was the only kingbird brought to the sanctuary that year, so he grew up without seeing others of his kind. A kingbird's common habitats were woods, groves, and orchards, which meant I couldn't release him in my backyard. I had to find just the right place for him—but not before he had practiced catching live prey. So that summer, I spent several evenings standing on a stepladder, picking off moths of the usual tiny brown variety that had gathered under the porch light, and confined them inside a shoebox for later emancipation in the outdoor cage. On one of those nights, I found a large gray moth with elaborate eye patterns on its wings, and the word "delicious" popped into my head, though by then I had been a vegetarian for over a decade. I'd been training the kingbird by dangling mealworms in front of him as he perched on a branch and then tossing the worms into the air. He'd become quite adept at grabbing them, but the little brown moths still often eluded him. Seeing him swoop down from his perch and snap up that beautiful, big moth was one of the most satisfying moments of my rehab career.

My kingbird learned to catch the small moths, too, but I wasn't sure if he would recognize an insect that didn't come out of a shoebox. Then, a birdwatcher friend spotted a family of kingbirds in the woods at the wildlife sanctuary that had two fledglings about the same age as mine and suggested it was time to let him go.

"Birds don't know how to count," my friend assured me. "The parents are still staying with their young. They'll think your bird is one of theirs and take him in."

He drew me a map, and I drove to the sanctuary with the fledgling perched on a branch inside a pet carrier. Once inside the gate, I parked my car and walked into the woods. In the clearing where my friend had seen the kingbirds, I set down the pet carrier, and my bird began to chirp. Almost instantly, an adult kingbird appeared on a branch overhead, flashing its white tail feathers like a handkerchief. I opened the pet carrier, and the fledgling flew out with no hesitation, and for a few minutes, I could hear the two birds rustling around in the thick foliage, calling to each other. I waited until all was quiet, apart from the buzzing of grasshoppers flying in low arcs in and out of the undergrowth, and then I picked up the empty pet carrier and walked away.

I knew that most of the birds I released would be dead before the year was out. To care too much about their individual fates would have been unnatural, even unkind. Kindness to wildlife means respecting their freedom. The goal of conservation is to save the species, not each individual bird. I had done everything I could to prepare that kingbird for survival. Just like my mother had done for me before she decided against surviving herself.

Bird rehabilitators are trained not to give names to the animals in their care or to talk *about* them or *to* them in sentimental language. I fed the baby birds entrusted to me in complete silence so they would not associate human voices with food,

Cat and Bird

and I resisted the urge to cuddle and pet them when I picked them up. But it was impossible not to become attached to the birds I spent weeks keeping alive. I could only steel myself against their likely fate because I had one animal I could possess and protect completely.

Dorian, my first Siamese cat, was eight weeks old when I met him at his breeder's house in 1979, my first year in graduate school. His name was inspired by his gray coloring and the Oscar Wilde seminar I was taking that semester, but like most Siamese kittens, he had very little fur; his long pinkish tail resembled a rat's. At our first meeting, Dorian left his sleeping siblings, sauntered over to me, and began rubbing his mouth against my finger. His lips were parted just enough to reveal his tiny teeth, sharp as dressmakers' pins, and he was purring. His whiskers trembled from the vibration as his wet gums slid back and forth. Though I didn't know as much about cats then as I do now, I realized he was marking me with his saliva, claiming me for his own. When I tried to pet him, he bumped his forehead against my palm over and over, and he wouldn't stop. He wanted to be the one to pet me, not the other way around. I was amazed by the sense of recognition that came over me. He was mine; I was his, and there was no going back.

My devotion to Dorian was instantaneous, all-exclusive, and everlasting, the way I imagined a mother's love must be for her children. He was a seal point Siamese, stockier and more violently committed to me than all four Siamese cats that would succeed him. He grew up to weigh fourteen pounds; his slightly crossed blue eyes peered out shrewdly from his dark brown face. The fur on his body became more beige than gray, but he was Dorian all right. People joked about the picture of him I must be hiding somewhere. He bit all my friends and actually drew blood, but he sat calmly in my lap while I brushed his teeth and trimmed his claws. That cat would have let me do anything to him just to spite the other people in my life. He needn't have bothered. When I was with Dorian, other people scarcely existed. Locked in our mutual possessiveness and insecurity, I demanded his absolute attention, and he demanded mine.

I didn't feel the same unwavering love for anyone else, though sometimes, when the nearly naked, lizard-like nestlings in the laundry baskets fluttered their bony wings and opened their mouths to me, I believed that satisfying their hunger was the most important thing in the world. Dorian didn't pay any attention to the birds I carried in and out of the house, but he'd always greet me at the door when I came in after releasing them. I'd pick him up, bury my face in his fur, and walk around the house, cradling him in my arms.

Living with pets is all about caring for specific individuals and keeping them safe. Before the word "pet" became popular in the late nineteenth century, a companion animal was referred to as a "favorite." A favorite dog or cat was an animal set apart from all the others of its kind by being given a name and being invited to live in the house as a member of the family. A hunting dog, no matter how valued, is a working animal, while a Yorkie smuggled into a black-tie reception inside a novelist's handbag is a pet— her favorite, her chosen plus-one. Dorian was my favorite. Caring for him wasn't just a moral or ethical obligation. I had made a permanent commitment to keep him happy and safe.

Dorian and I would go around inspecting all the rooms, putting away anything that could possibly hurt him: a piece of string, plastic bags, paper bags with handles that could wrap around his neck, glassware left too close to the edge of a table. And then I'd resume the same minor chores I did every day to make sure the birds would grow up and fly away. I almost never left my house but to pick up new nestlings, and even though I couldn't prevent the birds from perishing the same day they left my care, I was able to concentrate on the task at hand, being mindful of every detail. I was maintaining their wings in motion and holding on tight so I could eventually let them go. Meanwhile, Dorian was doing the opposite: he was leaving me alone so he could eventually have me all to himself. He didn't station himself outside the guest room, hissing and growling, when I was taking care of the baby birds—he only did that when my friends would spend the night in there and were afraid to come out.

My husband, Chuck, was actually afraid of birds, a fact I discovered early in our relationship when a starling and its fledgling ended up behind the dining room wall in the apartment we were renting. One morning, I came home from class just in time to see an adult bird fly out of the compartment into which our sliding pocket door disappeared. Dorian, who had been sitting nearby, remained in place, too stunned to chase a live toy. I picked him up, carried him to the bedroom, put him on the bed, and shut the door. By then, Chuck was chasing the bird all over the apartment, his head covered with the afghan that was usually draped over the back of the couch. He had opened all the windows and was trying to direct the bird outside.

Our apartment was in an old house, with sliding glass doors between the living room and the balcony. I ran across the living room to open those doors, and the starling soared through them. We couldn't see where it went, which meant the chirping we heard a few seconds later, growing louder and louder, was coming from behind the wall. We were afraid to slide the pocket door and crush the bird by accident, so we borrowed our neighbor's saw and cut a hole in one of the wall's wooden panels. We shone a flashlight into the opening and glimpsed a fledgling with peach fuzz on its head. It was chirping loudly, hopping between the exterior and the interior walls. I tried to coax it out with the sunflower seeds I had purchased to make vegetarian burgers, but every time I reached in, the bird hopped farther back. Since I had to return to school and teach another class, Chuck had to take over.

"Dorian can stay in the bedroom," I said to him. "Maybe the bird will come out, and you can catch him."

Three hours later, I came home to find Chuck sitting in a chair a few feet away from the cutout in the wall, holding a tennis racket.

"The bird keeps coming out, then hopping back in. The next time he jumps out, I'm going to block the hole with this."

Just as he said that, the bird emerged. Chuck sprang up and slammed the racket over the hole. Startled, the bird fled across the dining room toward the kitchen, hopping, then flying low, then landing, hopping, and flying again.

"Great, he knows how to fly," I said. "You can put him out on the balcony where the other one went. That must have been his mother."

I opened the balcony's glass doors once more to the astonishing clamor of countless winged creatures—like a stadium-sized orchestra of squeaky violins—that had gathered in the trees. I knew birds didn't abandon their young after a human had touched them, but here was a whole flock of starlings come to take care of its own. I ran back through the house and down the hallway outside our kitchen, where the fledgling was crouched in a corner, rocking on its feet and screeching at Chuck, who was holding a broom.

"Come on, buddy," Chuck said, reaching gingerly toward the bird with the bristles of the broom. "Let's go. I'm only trying to help."

The bird lunged at the broom, causing Chuck to stagger backward, and then flew into the kitchen, where it landed next to the stove. All of its feathers were puffed up, its beak wide open and shrieking. Every cornered animal is an embodiment of fear and desperation. If that bird was a cat, Chuck would have understood that the poor thing was hissing and growling and getting ready to pounce because it perceived his broom as a weapon. Even so, he was able to get the bird to turn around and hop-fly through the house onto the balcony. Immediately, several starlings landed next to the fledgling and guided it to its true identity in the trees, where dozens of others were waiting to reclaim it into the flock. The fledgling hop-flew to the higher branches and vanished among the leaves.

"You should have told me you were afraid to touch the bird. I thought you wanted to be the one to let it out, after waiting all those hours while I was at school."

"I don't like handling little animals," he said. "I'm afraid they're going to bite me and I'll freak out and squeeze them to death by mistake."

Thus began a new game that Dorian and I would play for years afterward called "Chuck and the Bird," in which I chased him around the house with a broom, calling out, "Take it easy, buddy. Don't bite me. I'm only trying to help."

All summer long, I'd shuttle between the birds and Dorian and the early lives of my stories. My first drafts were only a loose collection of impressions held together by a rudimentary plot. I'd return every day to a possibly doomed project and reread each sentence, then cross out, rephrase, add, and move words around. Writing was about survival, too. The draft that didn't get pitched into the trash would live to see another day. Maybe, after a dozen revisions, the hopelessly messy pages might cohere into something I could recognize: the right characters in the right places, and what happened to them, plausible but not predictable. I was well into one story when the main character began acquiring a pure-minded, all-or-nothing personality that was nothing like mine. I was only serious about four things— writing, running, Dorian, and birds. My character, however, took everything to heart. It was exhausting to spend so much time inside her head, untangling her knot of commitments, but trying to find the right words demanded my unique attention and ushered me into a kind of dream state. Several years out of graduate school by then, I preferred to work on my own. Only my editors read my stories.

My basement office had a cement floor covered by a black-and-white shag carpet that my friend Anne had stolen from our college dorm the night before graduation. A bare lightbulb hung from the two-by-fours nailed across the ceiling. No one except Dorian and I ever entered that room. He would sit on my desk and watch me work, leaning forward in a posture that reminded me of a gargoyle. He would actually growl if Chuck came down to do laundry, but he never followed me when I ran up the stairs every fifteen minutes to feed the birds. He seemed to understand I was coming right back and waited at his post, my writing's sole witness.

Dorian watched me write everything—from my graduate school thesis to my first published book. He was two when Chuck and I married, fifteen when we divorced. Writing about the marriage years later, I made it sound as if Dorian was a colorful minor character, a Siamese cat who terrorized everyone that stepped foot into our house, a cat who became my mascot. But the truth is more like this: between the ages of twenty-two and forty, I lived with a Siamese cat who loved me and hated everyone else. In the middle of his reign, Dorian at least became fond enough of my husband to sit in his lap if I wasn't home or to sleep on his chest till I, too, retired for the night, at which time the cat would walk across the bed, crawl under the covers into my arms, and put his head on my pillow. The animal in this revision is no mascot. He is my partner, the symbol and fortifier of my solitude.

Dorian recognized the sound of my car coming around the corner—according to Chuck—and ran to the foyer from wherever he was in the house. The moment I opened the door, he sprang forward to bump his head on my legs and then flop on the floor at my feet. He made no attempt to dash out, even if whatever I was carrying prevented me from closing the door behind me. I'd drop everything and pick him up, purring and clinging to me, then walk around the house, kissing him and talking to him in a squeaky voice. That was our ritual, our codependent sustenance. Stopped at a traffic light halfway home, I'd already be thinking of the warmth of his fur against my face. I couldn't wait to lift him into my arms and feel his satisfying, solid weight.

The unmitigated mutual regard of pet love would be creepy and wrong between humans. I could never tolerate the kind of attention I lavished on my cat. When I was newly in love with Chuck, I was often impatient for our visit to be over so I could mull over the details in private and decide how I really felt about him. Loving a human is largely mental and abstract. Not so with cats. I am always restored to myself when my arms are encircling their rounded backs or I'm burying my face in their fur, all of me in touch with whatever animates us alone, together.

After my summers became too busy and I had to stop volunteering at the bird sanctuary, I still needed solo activities to break up the hours at my desk. I spent many afternoons walking in the woods or riding my bicycle through the countryside. Sometimes Dorian and I would go for a drive. He enjoyed car rides so long as they didn't end up at the animal hospital or a new home we were moving into. The two of us would drive around town, measuring my running and cycling routes with the car's odometer. We'd stop in deserted parking lots to watch waterfowl in marshes and ponds from the car window, or we'd pull up at a drive-through and order fried cheese curds and hot fudge sundaes to take home. Dorian would sit calmly inside the pet carrier placed sideways on the passenger seat, accepting treats through its slatted metal door. All this changed when I lived with him on my own. Then, we didn't have to go anywhere. We could just sit on the couch, the two of us cocooned in silence, and be at our happiest.

I knew Chuck and I couldn't stay married once I fully accepted that I only felt like my true self when I was alone. I became a writer, in part, to justify all the hours I wanted to spend behind a locked door. The same need had drawn me to bird rehabilitation—meticulous, repetitive concentration requiring a singular, peaceful space: filling the syringe, shooting the formula into tiny mouths, cleaning feathers with a Q-tip, changing the paper lining of the berry boxes, putting each bird back into its berry box and each box back inside its laundry basket, the birds and me working together in unison behind my guest room's locked door. Still, I knew that caring for them meant respecting their essential nature and, sooner or later, I'd have to let them go. Our bond was temporary, and I was fine with that. It meant my work had succeeded.

But bird rehabilitation was a solo project. Its intimate human rewards came in raising and protecting another living creature, watching it grow, and then setting it free. Witnessing a bird's rebirth as it flew up and vanished in the gray light of dawn felt like something akin to faith. I had dedicated myself to the fierce desire of all living things to become what they were born to be. The journey had united me with a universal life force, and the personal rewards were all mine. I didn't need a future, or a past, or a husband.

Chapter Three

Lifting the Bones

The moment he heard my father's footsteps, Neko-chan, my mother's cat, would leave her side and flee to the nursery. My mother would check on me after serving tea to my father—or dinner if he was inclined to eat—and always find Neko-chan sleeping in my crib, his big gray head next to mine.

The fear of cats suffocating babies—"sucking their breath," as it's ominously phrased—must not have been prevalent in Japan in 1957. Takako, my mother, recalled the cat with great affection. His name, Neko-chan, meant "Kitty," a form of endearment appropriate for cats of any age and either gender. Seeing us together, our heads about the same size but the rest of the cat sprawled across the crib, had amused her.

"You were such a good baby," Takako always said. "You didn't cry like your brother did. Whenever I snuck in to check on you, you were sleeping peacefully with Neko-chan. You didn't even know I was there."

The nursery was upstairs; on the first floor were my parents' bedroom and the kitchen, where Takako waited up for Hiroshi, my father, who would come home well after midnight and leave at dawn. Neko-chan would sneak downstairs after he was gone to keep Takako company.

Neko-chan hated the camera. Maybe he was afraid of the sound of the shutter or the flash of light, but being photographed was the one thing he wouldn't do for her—so all I ever knew about what he looked like was his big gray head. He might have been a completely gray shadow of a cat or a tabby with gray and black stripes. The only people who would remember him now are my uncles, whom I haven't seen in nearly thirty years. As a child, I never thought to ask my mother for a better description of him, or why she didn't give him a more original name, or how he came to be her cat, or if she had raised him from the time he was a kitten. I didn't wonder about these details because the truth at the heart of the story eclipsed all else: Neko-chan hid in the nursery because he knew my father wouldn't set foot in there; I was not important to Hiroshi, but it didn't matter. I was born after my parents had stopped loving each other, and even a cat could tell my father was a liar and a cheat.

Neko-chan would come and go through an open window. Then one day, when I was two and could finally toddle around the house without holding on to my mother's hand, he left in the afternoon and didn't return that night. My mother and my uncles, Shiro and Kenichi, searched for days. Although Neko-chan had seemed healthy, Takako eventually concluded he had gone off to die. Neko-chan had been with her for ten years, since before she had married my father, when she was still sharing the house with my uncles. She never got another cat.

I first heard this story when I was five or six, just old enough to understand that I had a past about which stories could be told. I was aware of once being someone very different: a baby smaller than a cat, growing up in the same house where my mother had grown up in Kobe. There were pictures of her on the wall with her brothers and sisters in their school uniforms, posing in front of the gate. When I was five and my brother, Jumpei, was one, our family moved to a newly built suburban apartment complex. Kenichi occupied the old house after we left, and both Shiro and Keiko, their younger sister, settled nearby to raise their families. My mother would take us back there for visits. Year after year, in photographs of us with our cousins, the house in the background stood as proof of my mother's life before she had me. I realize now that the story of Takako's cat wasn't simply a masked tale about my father's betrayal and neglect. It was a parable to prepare me for a future without her.

One detail in the story continues to bother me. I didn't walk until I was two because my hips were dislocated at birth. As a breech baby whose mother had already suffered two miscarriages, I didn't breathe for an alarming number of seconds after I was born. The doctors must have been relieved I wasn't dead, but they didn't notice my hip injury for another few months. By then it had become much worse. I spent the next year and a half in a series of casts and braces that immobilized my legs. Shiro and Kenichi recalled that I had to be tethered like a puppy to keep me from crawling around the house and hurting myself. They were amazed I grew up to be a runner and cheered every race I won at school; to them, every medal was a miracle. So, I wonder, how could I have been such a good baby, one who never cried and slept so serenely, if I had dislocated hips and couldn't move? Surely I must have been in pain and constant turmoil, but the injury and my recovery are completely absent from my mind, along with all the hours I spent in the crib with the big gray cat. I always imagined Neko-chan jumping into a dark thicket and, with a flicker of his tail, taking all of my memories with him.

My parents met at the Kobe office of Kawasaki Steel, a manufacturing conglomerate where my mother was a secretary and my father an engineer. Her brothers saw right away that Hiroshi was arrogant. Her parents, who had moved back to the rice-farming village where the family was from originally, didn't trust his easy charm and tried to warn her against him. But Takako said she would rather die than marry anyone else. In 1954, when most couples had arranged marriages, theirs was a rare love match. By the time I was born three years later, my father was going out drinking every night and seeing a woman who worked as a bar hostess.

Like many Japanese mothers of the fifties and sixties, Takako believed that the most important thing she could give me and my brother was not security or comfort but discipline. She was told commercial baby formula was more nutritious than breast milk and babies should be fed with a bottle on a strict, predetermined schedule, not when they cried from hunger. Picking up and holding us when we fussed would only encourage us to cry harder each time we wanted attention. American mothers of her generation let their children cry themselves to sleep, too, but the emphasis on discipline must have resonated especially strongly in Japan, where *gaman,* stoic forbearance, was a cardinal virtue.

One of the few memories I have from the old house in Kobe is of hearing my brother cry in the nursery while I slept in my room across the hall. Some nights, Jumpei made so much noise that Hiroshi left the house. Over the baby's wails, I could hear my father slamming the front door. My mother would then come up the stairs, but she never stayed in the nursery very long. She would retreat down the steps while the baby continued to cry. Takako must have touched my brother's forehead to make sure he didn't have a fever, adjusted the covers, and steeled herself to walk away. I fell back asleep, and Jumpei wailed on while my mother lay awake, fretting for hours in her bedroom, her son refusing to sleep and her husband gone. Every night, until I was old enough to stay up with her, she would put me and my brother to bed in separate rooms and sit alone in the kitchen for hours, waiting for Hiroshi to come home.

I couldn't comprehend how difficult it must have been for her to let my brother cry himself to sleep until one of my friends in Boston became a mother. When I had dinner with her and her husband, my friend would jump up from the table and run to the nursery every time her daughter cried. She'd take the baby out of her crib and walk around the house, carrying her until she fell back asleep, only to repeat the whole thing in ten or twenty minutes when the baby cried again. Her husband had also deserted the table and was wandering around the house, trying to comfort both his wife and his child. Both of them knew that their daughter was healthy and safe, but their distress was palpable. The whole atmosphere crackled with the baby's cry.

And here my father had been free to walk out of the house in the middle of the night and (supposedly) stay at a hotel, while my mother could never leave the house by herself unless she was shopping for groceries, caring for a sick relative, or attending a PTA meeting at school. On weekends, when I was old enough to know how to be quiet in public places, she would take me on outings around town, leaving Jumpei with our aunts. Takako loved seeing beautiful things, but in order to visit a museum or a botanical garden, I had to go with her so she could claim she was providing an education for her daughter. Respectable women of her generation didn't go traipsing around town to amuse themselves. They pursued hobbies at home and socialized with neighbors. When my mother and her friends got together for tea, each woman brought her needlework so as not to sit idle.

I never saw my parents touching or talking in an affectionate way to each other. They were seldom in the same room in my memory. My father might as well have inhabited a separate galaxy. But what they had in common was their inability to be happy alone. Friends and family members alike talked about how Takako could light up a room by just walking in; even *my* friends vied for her attention and told me over and over, "Your mother is so pretty," "She is so kind and funny," "I love coming to your house."

Although I had no occasion to observe my father with his friends, my aunt—his sister—always said he was the life of the party wherever he went. The few times my brother and I went on outings with him, I could tell our father moved around the world with confidence, and people—especially women but men too—were drawn to him.

Both of my parents were charismatic extroverts, and I was the opposite. I looked forward to rainy days so I could play alone in my room. There was so much to occupy myself with: piles of books, some of them from the library, others my own; notebooks in which I wrote adventure stories and fairy tales and illustrated them with colored pencils; several sets of paper dolls—families from around the world, kings and queens, famous artists, and musicians—that I dressed and then mixed up deliberately so I could imagine what had brought the unlikely characters together. I was surprised when the day was over and it was time for dinner.

My mother loved me in an anxious, worrying way, and I responded like a Siamese cat, by attaching myself exclusively to her. But my relationship with her was more emotional than physical. Although I spent hours by her side, I hated being cuddled and petted, and I cried every morning when she tried to brush my hair because I couldn't stand having my head touched. Painfully ticklish, I recoiled when she placed her hand anywhere near my neck or shoulders. And yet on my first day at kindergarten, I ran away during recess and tried to find my way home. A posse of teachers found me wandering around the neighborhood like a lost kitten. Takako must have been saddened but relieved when I was finally old enough to ride my bike and use public transportation. Then I, too, started to roam. Still, however it made her feel, she always praised me for leaving the house to spend time with my friends.

I didn't know the details of my father's affair until 1994, after Hiroshi had died of cancer and the bar hostess, who hadn't been invited to the funeral, called my aunt's house and told her that he had telephoned her every day from the hospital until the afternoon of his death, when he was finally too sick to talk. I was surprised by Hiroshi's faithfulness to this woman, the first of his many girlfriends. After our family moved away from my mother's relatives, my father stopped coming home every night. Women would call our house looking for him. Long before I knew about sex, I understood all these women were his girlfriends.

I was ten and my mother thirty-nine when my parents bought a large two-story house in a quiet neighborhood. My father had been promoted to upper management by then. He worked late and traveled often, seldom telling us where he was going and when he was coming back. I would return from school in the late afternoon to find my mother sitting alone in the cold and dark kitchen. She said she was too tired to get up from the table to move to a sunnier room upstairs. The hobbies she'd pursued for years—embroidery, sewing, knitting, baking—no longer interested her. Our new house was up on a hill overlooking the rest of the city. In the winter, when the trees shed their leaves, my mother could almost see our old neighborhood three miles away, but she could not leave our house to visit her friends now that they were no longer neighbors.

Takako still waited up for Hiroshi on the nights he was supposed to be working in town. I did my homework in the kitchen to keep her company, but most nights, he called with some vague excuse for not coming home. My mother cried and said she was worried about my brother and me growing up and leaving her because without us, her life would be nothing. She wondered what she had done to drive Hiroshi away and berated herself for having been a failure as a wife.

"Promise you won't be like me," she kept saying. "You are smart and strong. You can't end up like me."

A week after my twelfth birthday, Takako asked Hiroshi to take my brother and me on a rare Sunday outing. We came home and found her on the floor with the gas pipe in her hand and all the windows sealed shut. My father should have called an ambulance instead of an old family friend who was a surgeon. My mother had stopped breathing; her skin was cold to the touch. Still, Hiroshi was less concerned about saving her than he was about protecting himself from blame. The police he summoned afterward allowed him to report the death as an accident.

My father was careful to plan a proper Buddhist wake and funeral for Takako, even though, like most Japanese families of the era, our family seldom visited temples or shrines. Our relatives, his coworkers, and my mother's friends, all dressed in black, gathered at our house for the two-day ritual. In the living room, the furniture and walls were covered in billowy white drapes; two monks from a Buddhist temple burned incense and chanted sutras in front of her coffin, which was wrapped in white cloth. My cousins, who were four and five, cried whenever the chanting grew louder. The monks' two voices rising and falling like groans of pain were interrupted by sudden gasps for breath. Their words, slurred and droned, weren't meant to be understood. If this was the language of the dead, I thought, I would never be able to speak to my mother if she came back as a ghost.

At the end of the second day, the coffin was opened. Dressed in a white burial kimono, my mother still looked like herself, with the light makeup she had worn to visit museums and dress shops with me. Her best friend, our neighbor from the apartment complex, was standing next to me. She and my mother could only talk on the phone once they were separated; the three miles between their houses might as well have been an ocean. Maybe she meant to comfort me, but she cried even harder than I did. Years later, she would tell me that this was the moment she realized my mother had succumbed from the malady of being a good wife.

Only eight of us rode in the black limousine that followed the hearse to the crematorium: my father, his father and sister, my mother's parents, her two brothers, and me. Together, we represented the two sides of my mother's family. Jumpei stayed behind at the house with the other children. I didn't understand why he was too young to come with us until I was in the crematorium, witnessing her coffin sliding into the chute. Then we waited a long time in a sparsely furnished sitting room before being called back into the crematorium chamber to stand around a steel table that held a mound of white ashes.

The fire had devoured almost all of my mother's body, but a pair of thigh bones was still discernable. At one end of the table was a white urn and a tray of steel chopsticks twice their usual length. Two by two, opposite sides of the family took turns raising the bone fragments with the chopsticks and passing them from person to person to place inside the urn. We started with the bones of her feet and then moved up the body to fragments of her skull, so that my mother could walk upright on her journey to the land of the dead. My father picked up the first bone with his chopsticks and motioned for me to lift mine. He—the head of our family—was passing the bone to me, the oldest child. I did not want to believe that the cracked gray chip between my chopsticks had anything to do with my mother's feet that used to walk with me through the botanical gardens. My aunt kept looking at me in a worried way. If she, or any other adult in that room except my father, had been in charge, I would not have been standing inside a crematorium chamber at the age of twelve, assembling my mother's incinerated bones.

For my maternal grandparents and uncles, this was their final goodbye. They had given Takako up to my father's family, once in marriage and now in death. The urn was buried in a gloomy garden at a temple in Osaka. The grave marker, a tall granite column, was engraved with the names of my father's ancestors going back several generations. My mother's family had to abandon her there among the bones of dead people she was related to only by marriage, none by blood.

Later, I would learn from Buddhist friends that the ritual at the crematorium was called *kotsu-age*, "lifting the bones." The bones were raised in tandem with family members using two pairs of chopsticks to symbolize how the living must console one another and come together to honor the dead. I could only imagine the life my mother might have had if my father had cared for her as carefully as he had lifted her bones from the pile of white ashes.

Chapter Four

Re-Homed

Hiroshi moved one of his girlfriends into our house a few weeks after my mother's death and married her before the year was out. But his philandering didn't stop. My stepmother, Michiko, would pack her bags and threaten to leave whenever he spent too much time with the bar hostess he couldn't marry because her job was too scandalous.

Michiko met my father when he was staying at a business hotel managed by her parents. Having worked in the family business for as long as she could remember, she was something of a professional housekeeper. After she married my father and he resumed his nightly excursions, Michiko remained at home and kept the premises spotless: every day she swept, vacuumed, dusted, and mopped. She wasn't much of a cook. She spent most of her time in the kitchen, picking up the few crumbs that fell on the floor or wiping off the scarcely visible stains that drove her to distraction. She refused to teach me how to do anything around the house, but I didn't care. By then I was certain that becoming a homemaker either killed you or turned you into a crazy, bitter person.

Everything became my fault. Michiko claimed that I made her miserable by failing to show her proper respect. Then, Hiroshi would beat me to prove his love to her and threaten to kill me if I drove her away. He would grab me by the hair and yank me down on the floor to beg for her forgiveness. Words I didn't mean came out of my mouth in a contorted, choked-up voice. Michiko always relented once my father made me cry. For a few weeks afterward, he would come home earlier and spend his evenings with her. But soon enough, he'd start staying out again, and then, inevitably, he would return late one night to find her sitting in the kitchen with her bags packed. They would argue for a few minutes, and then he would come stomping into my room, drag me downstairs, and hit me in front of her. It made no sense for my father to prove his love to her this way. It wasn't as though she was jealous of his love for me.

My father never felt bad about hurting me. He just came and went, taunting Michiko with his outside adventures, which in turn caused her to lash out at me. She had cleverly manipulated the situation so she didn't have to beat me herself; she could get Hiroshi to do it. My brother, who was eight at the time, stayed in his room—either sleeping or listening to music—while the rest of us raged and cried. I didn't have the luxury of shutting out the world by closing the door and turning up the volume on my stereo. I tried to render myself invisible, but the effort was useless; I couldn't lock my door, so I had no choice but to get dragged down the stairs to my own beating.

Michiko knew that my father and I didn't like, much less love, each other. He hadn't loved my mother either, and yet Michiko was determined to erase all traces of Takako's existence. She threw out the dresses my mother had made for me, the tapestries she had embroidered, the framed photographs of her in my room— all objects Hiroshi never noticed but to be irritated by them. Michiko's jealousy and insecurity were not logical, but her malice toward me knew no bounds. Alone in my room, I daydreamed, read, and wrote stories and diary entries in notebooks I hid under the carpet, but I knew the only safe space in the house was locked inside my head; at least no one could throw away my thoughts. Anything that could be discovered and tampered with, I would write in English, a language neither Michiko nor Hiroshi could read or understand. Takako had sent me to an American neighbor's house to learn English when I was nine, conceivably planning for my future without her even then. If she came back to me in a dream or as a ghost, I decided, we could communicate with each other in English, the secret language of my thoughts and feelings. Surely her spirit would be able to understand the words she never learned in real life.

Jumpei and I grew up like two bird species that coexisted in overlapping territories, each of us filling the niche left unoccupied by the other. He took to Michiko immediately after Takako's death, and suddenly, our roles reversed. He lingered in the kitchen after dinner, keeping Michiko company while she waited up for Hiroshi, and I fled to my room. The conversations they had were nothing like the ones I had with my mother when I sat up with her. Even with my door closed, I could hear them chatting and laughing. On the nights Michiko staged her confrontations, she would send Jumpei to his room so he wouldn't have to witness what was about to happen. My brother never mentioned the packed bags or the fights. He must have heard some of the yelling and crying, but he never asked me about it. He would grow up thinking of Michiko as his only mother and remember our years with her as a happy time. On the one occasion I brought up how Hiroshi had beaten me to appease her, Jumpei said, "Our father was a terrible father," and then he changed the subject.

My mother knew her death would be harder on me than

Cat and Bird

on my brother. Widowed men of Hiroshi's generation didn't have children in their second marriage if they already had a son from the first. And so my brother's place as the family's male heir was secure. As a girl, I could only benefit the family through an arranged marriage to someone whose business or family connections were useful to my father. Even if she had stayed alive, Takako couldn't have protected me from being married off and becoming another unhappy wife; the only way she could save me was to convince me that I didn't need a mother or a future husband. By praising me over and over for being strong and independent, she taught me that I could take care of myself. She couldn't have foreseen Hiroshi marrying a woman who treated me with utter hostility, but even if she had, my mother would have believed I had it in me to find my way out.

What went on in that house for eight years after her death was like a desperate catfight that could only be resolved by getting rid of one of the combatants. Years later, I would read about house cats turning on each other when one of them got out, roamed around, and came back: the remaining cats often attacked each other instead of the one that had strayed. By the time I left, I was the cat who got "re-homed" rather than mangled to death.

Chapter Five

He and I

My mother couldn't guide me toward a profession to ensure my financial independence because, except for the owner of her favorite dress shop, and my third-grade teacher, Miss Yoshida, she had never met a woman who supported herself. An unmarried woman from an upper-middle-class family like ours remained at home for life and was called *Ojosan*, "honorable daughter," even after her parents' deaths. The women from whom my friends and I took piano, watercolor, and calligraphy lessons were *Ojosan* in their forties. If I didn't marry, I too would lead a life of forced idleness, teaching genteel hobbies to other people's children for pocket money, dependent on my father and, later, my brother for all else.

A month before her suicide, Takako took me to Kobe College, a private bilingual academy for girls that included secondary school and a college, and enrolled me in junior high. The school was founded in 1875 by Eliza Talcott and Julia Elizabeth Dudley, two Congregational missionaries from Rockford, Illinois, who wanted to introduce young Japanese women to Christianity, but by the time I attended, it was better known for its English, music, and arts education. The daily services were more for music appreciation—our chapel had the largest pipe organ in the country—and the few required religion classes were taught by an American-educated theologian whose favorite writers were Søren Kierkegaard and Paul Tillich. The majority of the college graduates had arranged marriages with more cosmopolitan versions of their fathers, men who sought well-educated wives to accompany them on their overseas assignments, but others moved abroad to work for global companies or government agencies. Leaving the country was the only way a woman could earn her own living without embarrassing her family. My mother must have thought continuing with bilingual education was my best chance of escaping a doomed marriage.

Six years after Takako's death, as I approached my high school graduation, I still had no idea how I would ever support myself. I had no aptitude for business or politics. Being fluent in English was my only practical skill, but I couldn't picture myself working in an office or traveling all over the world on assignment. I was at my happiest staying in my room, reading and writing. So I remained on campus to attend the college, and after two years of studying English and American literature, I received a scholarship to finish my bachelor's degree in the United States at Rockford College, the founders' alma mater. None of the American teachers or exchange students I knew at Kobe College had been to Rockford, but I didn't care. Once I left Japan, I had no intention of returning.

On the morning of my departure, I came downstairs with my suitcase to see my father smoking at the kitchen table and Michiko standing at the counter, scrubbing the sink. He was wearing a suit and tie; she, a housedress. Hiroshi usually left for work around seven, but it was now past ten, so I figured he had delayed his departure to speak to me. I sat down, though he didn't invite me to.

The ashtray had several cigarette butts, a few with traces of my stepmother's lipstick on them. I wondered how long they'd been smoking and waiting. My father took another puff from his cigarette and asked me, "If I die while you are in America, will you come back for the funeral?"

We had never discussed how long I would be gone, but of

course they knew they might never see me again. My father wasn't likely to die anytime soon, so maybe asking the question was his way of acknowledging my escape from him. But he could also have been gauging my level of disrespect even after his death. Either way, I didn't want to lie, so I said, "Probably not."

My father squinted hard at me. "If you get into trouble in America, we have no choice but to take you back because we're your family. I hope you know that."

He didn't wait for me to respond. He put out his cigarette, got up from the table, and walked out of the kitchen. Michiko ran after him, still in her housedress, to drive him to the commuter train station as she did every morning. After she left, Jumpei came down to the kitchen on his way to the nearby country club, where he drove golf carts in exchange for lessons. He picked up the thermos of iced tea Michiko had prepared for him and turned to go.

"Bye," we said to each other with a little nod and a wave.

Michiko returned and changed into slacks and a blouse. She had told me the night before that she would accompany me in a taxi to the airport so my friends who'd be there to see me off would not tell their parents that she had failed to send me off in a proper manner. I hadn't told my friends about my troubles at home because I didn't think they would understand. Besides, when I was with them, I just wanted to forget about my homelife. Michiko was so unlike my friends' mothers, none of whom smoked or wore makeup around the house, but they would never gossip about her with their parents because she wasn't important to them. Soon, she wouldn't be important to me, either.

Michiko turned to me while the taxi driver was putting my suitcase into the trunk and said, "Your father is glad that you're leaving. But he's worried about the future. We won't be able to find you a husband if you come back. No Japanese family will want a daughter-in-law who has spent two years living in a dorm with foreigners."

"You don't have to worry about me," I said.

Except for Michiko exchanging pleasantries with the driver, we didn't talk during the thirty-minute ride to the airport. I was relieved she had decided to call a taxi rather than driving me herself. I'd had visions of her crashing the car and killing us both, just to keep me from making a clean getaway.

A dozen friends from school were waiting for me at the airport. My mother's best friend—the one who had cried in front of the coffin—had come too. Michiko stood apart from the rest of us as we said goodbye, all of us tearing up. I had gone to see my grandparents and uncles the weekend before at my grandparents' house in the country. These were the people I wanted to remember, even though they too would fall away from my life once I boarded the plane.

After hours of air travel, layovers, and customs lines, the last leg of my journey was a ninety-minute bus ride from Chicago's O'Hare Airport to downtown Rockford. The stretch of farmland, with an enormous sky brooding over it, looked utterly dismal. I arrived at dusk. A volunteer from the student life office picked me up at the bus station, and we drove past supermarkets, convenience stores, a scattering of restaurants and bars, and a motel designed to look like a Swiss chalet. The campus was on the edge of town, set back in the woods down a long, winding road from the main gate. This was about as far away as I could be from my father's house on a hill, famous for its "million-dollar view" of sparkling neon signs and the scalloped coastline of Osaka Bay. At least no one from my family could blame me, hit me, or threaten to kill me anymore.

Rockford College had six hundred students, most of whom lived on campus. Although I had met all of them by the time the first semester was over, I became close friends with only three women: two fellow English majors with whom I shared creative writing classes, worked at the library's reference desk, and edited the student literary magazine, and an art major who worked on the magazine's graphics. The English majors shared a double room in the new residence hall with more amenities, but I had chosen the old dorm with cinder block walls so I could have a single room. And despite being thousands of miles and an ocean away from Kobe, my daily routine remained surprisingly the same. Aside from classes, the library, and hanging out with my new friends, I spent hours alone, running, swimming, or reading and writing in my room. Unlike my teachers back home, who all assumed I would either marry or work for a global company, my teachers at Rockford encouraged me to go to graduate school and become a writer.

At the start of my junior year, I began writing character sketches of slightly eccentric people engaged in ordinary activities, like drinking tea. My creative writing professor, Dr. Trafton, said I had "a way with words" and an eye for quirky details, but my sketches were too thin and whimsical. I created "interesting" characters who were only meant to be admired from a distance. He pushed me to write a story in which something actually happened, some conflict or trouble that changed a character's life. I still remember the phrase he used: "a full-fledged story." He must have sensed that my writing was trying to hatch out of its shell and grow into an avian life-form that could fight for its continued existence.

Cat and Bird

During my senior year, my characters finally evolved into people with real emotions pitched against one another: a woman who walked out on a date to hitchhike home, two girls arguing under a frozen tree because only one of them would admit how much she cared for the other. I was learning how to write about risk, but I wasn't ready to work on my own. I applied to a PhD program in Milwaukee because the city was a relatively short drive away and it would give me five more years of study; as long as I stayed in school, my visa would be valid. Having moved such a long way from Japan, I wanted to stay within reasonable proximity of Rockford, and even though I had never taught a class in my life, I was accepted and given a fellowship to teach writing. Here finally was a way to support myself: showing people how to do the one thing I did, thought about all the time, and, perhaps with luck, could learn to talk about.

I took a Greyhound bus from Rockford to Milwaukee in late April and found an apartment through a "roommate-wanted" ad on the student union bulletin board: "Top floor of a 4-story brownstone. No elevator. The room, the smallest of 3, has its own bathroom, with a tub large enough for a midget." I thought: *Five foot two and barely one hundred pounds, I'm close.*

I moved in the day after graduation. Aside from the door that led to the minuscule bathroom, the room was set up almost exactly the same way as my dorm room and my bedroom at my parents' house, with a dresser against one wall, a daybed against the other, and a desk by the window. They were all the same size and furnished similarly, and in each location, I covered my bed with an Indian cotton print depicting the tree of life that I had purchased in Kobe when I was thirteen. I got a summer job at a restaurant, and for the next three months, I seldom left my room except to run and waitress.

My two roommates had grown up in a suburb and moved to Milwaukee together to attend college. Dan, whose red hair kept falling into his green eyes, was a graduate student in zoology. Larry, who had long black hair and a beard, worked as a counselor at a home for wayward teens. I was only a few years younger than they were, but they carried an impressive air of world-weariness about them. They'd spend whole afternoons smoking pot and listening to Frank Zappa. The coffee table was covered with zoology textbooks and books by Hunter S. Thompson. On Sunday mornings, after their weekend parties, I'd find a dozen men and women passed out on the floor of the living room, foyer, and hallway.

Although the kitchen was right outside my door, I dashed into it only to make coffee before hurrying back to my room. Half the space in the refrigerator was taken up by a beer keg, so I kept my food in a dorm-sized refrigerator in my room that I bought with my waitressing tips. I lived on peanut butter, applesauce, and cottage cheese. I avoided going into the pantry, where in one of the drawers, I found three vacuum-sealed plastic bags containing fetal pigs. Dan had stolen them from the zoology department, and sometimes he brought one out to use as a centerpiece. Right before their parties, I'd stock my fridge with everything I might possibly need, as though I was preparing for a natural disaster.

Two years after leaving my father's house, I was still trying to take up as little space as possible, still trying not to call attention to myself. And I might have remained in that self-contained room—my own tiny bomb shelter—for years if it hadn't been for the two cats who stayed with us in September while their owner,

Cat and Bird

Larry's sister, was moving from one apartment to another and didn't want the cats to get in the way.

Mabel was a large calico who sat on the couch all day. She was sweet, but it was Angus I adored—the skinny, all-black cat who drew me out of hiding. Angus took immediate possession of the apartment, and when I followed him from room to room, he was the active, bold part of me moving freely through a territory larger than I had ever allowed myself to claim. He was one-tenth my size, but I orbited around him like a satellite in an ever-expanding universe. His favorite trick was to bump my arm with his head just as I was raising my cup to my lips, causing me to spill my coffee. He did this just so I would yell out his name, put down the cup, and chase him around the apartment. He was incredibly fast. Though I was a decent sprinter for a human, I could never catch him. At a certain point, he would stop, flop on his back, pump his legs, and purr like crazy while I scratched his stomach. When he'd had enough, he'd twist his neck and bite my hand. The next moment, he was streaking across the room again with me in pursuit. Petting Angus until it animated him was like having sparks of electricity flow through my fingertips and surge into his fur. Or maybe it was the other way around. The current passed back and forth between us.

I started reading in the living room so I could periodically get up to chase Angus through the kitchen and up and down the long hallway. At night, I left my door ajar. Mabel would rouse herself from the couch around 3:00 a.m. Then she and Angus would race around my room, batting at each other and using the bed, with my body in it, as a fort. Because Larry often worked the night shift at the home for troubled teens, I offered to feed the cats. I moved their litter box out of his bathroom and into mine so I could clean it regularly. I couldn't fathom why anyone complained about this minor chore; it was so much easier than dragging huge bags of human garbage down four flights of stairs once a week.

Soon, I stopped sneaking around the apartment like a squatter. If the volume on the TV or the stereo was up too loud, I'd ask my roommates to turn it down. I began demanding my rights to the common space: the kitchen with an oven that actually worked, the living room with large windows overlooking the city, the long hallway where I ran with Angus. At last I was settling into my first apartment. And then, one October afternoon, I returned from school and found a note from Larry's sister on the plant stand by the door. Her new apartment was ready, so she had taken the cats home. They were gone.

I put the note back and walked into the living room. The air in the apartment felt not just quiet but dead. A week later, when I couldn't stand that feeling anymore, I told my roommates I planned to get my own cat.

"Cool," Larry said. "You should get a Siamese. They're affectionate and playful. My sister thinks Angus might be part Siamese."

I found Dorian through an ad that his breeder had placed in the *Milwaukee Sentinel*:

"Purebred Siamese kittens. Fifty dollars. First come, first served."

The following afternoon, I skipped a mandatory seminar for all new teaching assistants and took a series of buses—the ride was so long that my transfer expired twice—to the home of the breeder, Mrs. Pookay ("like bouquet," she said on the phone), on the south side of Milwaukee. Dorian wasn't ready to come home with me yet, but Mrs. Pookay and her husband drove him to my apartment when he was weaned. He arrived on the first day of December, just in time for the holiday season.

The first thing we did was sleep together. My daybed—which I'd inherited from the former occupant of my room—was tilted to the side, and it sagged in the middle. I couldn't sit on it without slouching into a semi-recumbent position. I put Dorian on my bed and lay down to pet him. When I woke up, my body was aslant across the mattress, my legs and arms tangled in the old tree of life bedspread. I'd been trying to hold up my head because Dorian had nestled under my chin. I struggled to reposition myself without crushing him or rolling off the bed, and then he woke up and clung to my neck with his paws. In the few hours we were asleep, I had gone from sleeping with Neko-chan, the cat of my infancy, to sleeping with Dorian in a new life that needed its own origin story. The kitten pressed his head against me and purred, transferring the vibrations from his tiny skull to my throat. My whole being became his personal amplifier. I cupped my hand around his body and pictured us on a raft, crossing a lake with no distant shore in sight.

I wasn't in the apartment when Dorian climbed the Christmas tree that Larry had set up in the living room, but I could picture him batting down the glass ornaments and releasing their internal pockets of air. I should have been more contrite on my new pet's behalf, but I didn't realize that someone whose favorite book was *Fear and Loathing in Las Vegas* would be sentimental about Christmas tree ornaments. One moment, Larry was yelling that I should take Dorian back to Mrs. Pookay, and the next, I was calling a listing for a new apartment. It turned out that the broken ornaments had belonged to Larry's grandparents. Still, he did not have the right to demand that I get rid of my cat. When I left my father's house, I'd sworn never again to live with someone who threatened me, so by the end of the week, Dorian and I had our own place.

In the one-room studio I rented, the sink, fridge, and stove were crammed into one corner, but they belonged only to me. I didn't have to clean up a roommate's mess or worry about my stepmother carrying on because I'd left a smudge on the sink after pouring myself a glass of water. I didn't really know how to cook, but my mother had taught me how to bake. In the years before she began crying every night, the two of us would spend long afternoons and evenings baking recipes from around the world. We made everything from cakes, pies, sourdough baguettes, and croissants to bagels and bialys. I knew what it meant when a recipe said that the dough should stop sticking to the board and look shiny, or that the loaf should sound hollow when you tapped it. Takako had shown me how to press pie dough from the center out and wrap it around the rolling pin for transfer to the baking tin. It was so satisfying when the circles fit perfectly to make the two halves of the pie.

People often say that cats only love us for their own selfish reasons while dogs are motivated by genuine loyalty. I suppose Dorian loved me because I was the most recognizable feature of his territory and the provider of his food, but I didn't expect anyone, human or animal, to love me for no reason. I wasn't interested in whether Dorian had true affection for me or if he just found me convenient. The more interesting question was how he had domesticated *me*. Even when Dorian scratched the couch and the carpet, spilled food and water around his bowls, scattered litter every time he jumped in and out of the box, he was also training me to clean the litter box, wash his bowls, and put away my clothes, books, dishes, and anything else he might chew, scratch, or break. He taught me to keep our home tidy but not spotless, a place where we could relax and be ourselves together. My favorite way to spend the evening was to be alone, cooking with him. I loved sitting down with him to eat all the wrong foods at all the wrong times: half a pear pie for dinner at 3:00 a.m., leftover soup for breakfast, scrambled eggs any time of day.

I was also finally making friends. I even had the makings of a social life with a dozen other graduate students. We'd walk over to the diner near campus after class to drink coffee and perform a postmortem on whose comments were brilliant or stupid, whose work received a fair critique and whose didn't. We started having weekly potluck dinners at a dilapidated house shared by two poets—Keith, who was from a Chicago suburb, and Nell, who was originally from Northern Ireland but had been raised by Protestant missionaries in Panama.

None of us could call ourselves a good cook. The charred chicken wings that Keith made on his tiny hibachi drove me to give up eating meat altogether. The casseroles I made from *Diet for a Small Planet* were often dry and bland, but at least they were edible. The most popular of my contributions was a seven-layer salad for which I substituted hearts of palm for fried bacon. That recipe, slathered with a cup of mayonnaise and topped with thawed-out green peas and shredded Swiss cheese, wasn't fit for a small planet, even without the bacon. It came from a pamphlet I found at a sidewalk sale compiled by "Martha's Circle" at a suburban Methodist Church. It was Nell's favorite, and I promised to make it for her twenty-sixth birthday, but I left it to the last minute and couldn't find fresh spinach for the first layer anywhere. Nell was furious and wrote me a long letter about how I had let her down and gone back on my promise. She was not the only one of my graduate school friends who could write a three-page, single-spaced letter about a seven-layer salad and make me feel like I'd committed a crime, but she forgave me after I cried so pitifully at the diner that the waitress was afraid to refill our coffee cups.

Nevertheless, I felt safe with them. It was the first time I'd had friends with whom I could talk about all of my childhood troubles, knowing that nothing in my past could possibly shock them. Linda, who had lost her mother at sixteen, had married her high school boyfriend simply because he had known her mother. Matt had a scar on his thigh from a cigarette his grandfather had put out on him, a punishment for wearing shorts when he was twelve. Nell's congregation used to pray over her to keep her pure—some in English, some in Spanish, and still others in "tongues."

Their stories emboldened me not only to talk about my family but to write short stories about them. I wanted to imagine how my grandmother might have experienced my mother's suicide, or what my mother was thinking in her last moments. The character based on me, the daughter who survived her mother's death, was a runner too, but she dreamed of becoming an artist rather than a writer. In life, it had been my mother, not me, who made watercolor sketches of the flowers in our garden, who remarked how the gladioli in the foreground of Monet's painting were taller than the woman— his wife—holding her green parasol in the upper-left-hand corner. Going back to my past in writing was like entering my own house through an attic window. By letting the daughter in my stories see and do what my mother had seen and done in our life together, I could become both my mother and myself on the page. The real-life stories that had seemed so depressing and boring at once suddenly acquired a new shine, the way other people's possessions might appeal to a thief. I had become an

Cat and Bird

intruder in the house of my past, a cat burglar of memory; in every room, I found something I could use.

I met Chuck during my third year of graduate school through my classmate George; they were sharing an apartment half a block away from mine. One night after class, George and I were drinking coffee in his kitchen when a skinny guy carrying an amp and a bass guitar walked in through the front door wearing jeans, a wrinkled T-shirt, and a bandana as a headband. George had been telling me for the second time about his debutante girlfriend who had broken his heart.

"Hey," the skinny guy said, addressing both me and George, even though he and I hadn't met. "I just got done with rehearsal." Then he looked at me and laughed, "It's a wedding band. Nothing special." And for the rest of the night, we talked as if I was one of his roommates. He was twenty-eight, three years older than I was. After nine years of college off and on, he'd finally settled on getting a degree in education; he wanted to teach elementary school. In the interim, he supported himself by painting houses, working on construction crews, and playing in a handful of lounge and wedding bands. Even though he only sang occasional backup harmony, he knew the lyrics to crowd favorites like "Twist and Shout," "Your Cheating Heart," and "Proud Mary."

I had never met anyone who was so confident and self-deprecating at the same time. Chuck was a paradox: a laid-back rebel who refused to do anything he considered stupid or pointless and laughed about it instead of getting worked up with indignation. For the next few months, we went running together every day after school. My graduate school friends came across as moody, thin-skinned, and melodramatic by comparison. Maybe I needed a break from them, I thought. And a few months later, Chuck and I moved in together.

Dorian bit Chuck on their first encounter and then gradually eased up on open hostility. I knew that even if Dorian reverted to his territorial behavior after we moved in together, Chuck never would expect me to give him up. Like me, he hated people telling him what to do and was determined to let others be in return. Once inside our new apartment, I set Dorian's pet carrier in the spare room I intended to use as a study. But when I unlatched the carrier door, Dorian made a beeline for the closet, where the movers had left my clothes on the floor, still on their hangers. He crouched behind the clothes while I hung them up, thoroughly uninterested in exploring the rest of the house, so I set up his litter box and his food and water bowls nearby. Eventually, I crawled into the closet and lay down on the floor next to him, and the two of us fell asleep under the canopy of hanging clothes that reminded me of a forest. We had become prehistoric cave dwellers. Our bond would remain primal—and primary—no matter who we lived with.

For the next few days, Dorian would come out of the closet to watch me unpack my books and set up my desk, but he wouldn't leave the room, which now had most of things we had in our studio. When he finally ventured into the living room, he hopped from rug to couch to plant stand, assiduously avoiding any piece of furniture that was new to him. I coaxed him onto the chairs from Chuck's old apartment by covering them with my towels and blankets and then sitting there myself, giving him a treat when he jumped into my lap.

We lived in that apartment for two years while I finished my creative writing dissertation—a collection of short stories, some of which became the basis for my novel. They had a long way to go before they could be published, but completing my degree qualified me for a full-time, tenure-track teaching job. Ironically, the best offer came from a private college just outside Green Bay, Wisconsin—Chuck's hometown.

"Of course I'm moving to Green Bay with you. It would be really weird to have you living in my hometown without me," he said.

I accepted the offer and then discovered that despite the college's willingness to sponsor me for a work visa, the process was not simple: apparently, being selected for a job out of nearly two hundred applicants wasn't enough proof for the INS to believe that I was preeminently qualified. Both the college and I would need to hire attorneys; I might have to leave the country for a few months until my work visa was approved.

"We should just get married," Chuck said.

Chuck and I had always talked about marriage as an outdated institution. But we agreed it was outrageous for the government to put me through so much hassle before I could take a job that had been offered to me. Compared to the immigration and naturalization process, marriage was utterly benign. In fact, getting married seemed like the only logical next step, another act of rebellion, a shortcut to boycotting an unfair system. Chuck and I were like people in rural areas who often insisted they never made a decision to get a cat; a stray cat just decided to come and live with them. We got married because we were already living together; our immigration rebellion was a joint venture and also the path of least resistance. But what we shared more than anything was the wish to "do our own thing" and be left alone, which even Dorian could find himself supporting.

My favorite essay about marriage, "He and I," by the Italian novelist Natalia Ginzburg, begins with a simple, irreconcilable incompatibility: "He always feels hot, I always feel cold." She recounts how she and her husband disagreed about everything—food, music, art, the management of their finances—and how they bullied each other at every turn. Even though there are hints of affection in the way she makes fun of him, it's hard not to wonder how two people so unsuited to one another could have fallen in love and gotten married.

In the essay's last section, Ginzburg reveals that she and her husband had met once in their youth, but the idea of marrying him at the time was "light years from" her mind. They lost touch with each other and married when they met again years later. She doesn't tell us what drew them to each other the second time. Instead, she describes their first meeting, twenty years previously, as "two people who conversed so politely, so urbanely, as the sun was setting: who chatted a little about everything perhaps and about nothing; two friends talking, two young intellectuals out for a walk; so young, so educated, so uninvolved, so ready to judge one another with kind impartiality; so ready to say goodbye to one another forever, as the sun set, at the corner of the street."

Finally, in this last sentence, we realize what Ginzburg has been suggesting all along: marriage isn't even remotely about getting along with each other. When you love someone, you take to heart everything he says and does. You can't stand that he has his own mind and doesn't do what you want him to do. You long to control him, so you nag, cry, make sarcastic remarks, act in a passive-aggressive manner, or all of the above, and he does the same. People who love each other are honest with each other. They are not afraid to disagree and to fight.

Ginzburg was born in Sicily in 1916 and published her first novel in 1942 under a pseudonym because of the laws restricting publication by Jewish citizens under the German occupation. Her first husband, Leone Ginzburg, who led a clandestine anti-fascist movement, was arrested and died in prison from extreme torture. The man she wrote about in "He and I" was her second husband, Gabriele Baldini. In spite of the tragedy she suffered, many of her essays are ironic and humorous. The way she makes fun of her husband in "He and I" is similar to how comedians portray their spouses: the wife who nags, the husband who won't let you spend money, the crazy person you have to put up with. In both Ginzburg's work and in popular comedy routines, the stories about the wife or the husband are reassuring; we are, none of us, perfect, and we all need someone to love. The crazier the spouse, the stronger the attachment that holds the couple together, despite their unreasonable demands.

At holiday gatherings in Green Bay, the men in Chuck's family drifted to the basement or the den after dinner to watch whatever sport was on TV. The women would clean up the table and then gather in the kitchen to embark upon their husband stories: the husband burned the casserole he was trying to reheat; the husband's stinginess caused the wife to hide her expensive new dress in the guest room. These stories declared that the wives were needed, harassed, and, therefore, loved, or that they loved their husbands enough to tolerate their annoyances. I couldn't imagine talking about Chuck in this way. Did that mean I didn't love him?

Chuck and I weren't polar opposites like the husbands and wives in the holiday stories or Ginzburg's essay. Although our opinions didn't match up completely, we were more alike than we were different. Neither of us could balance a checkbook or figure out how to operate the new electronics gear we were obliged to purchase when an old machine couldn't be repaired, and he didn't burn casseroles any more than I did. We each had our own bank account and didn't care how the other spent his or her money. Being childless, we didn't have many big decisions to make together. It never occurred to us to depend on each other for things we couldn't do on our own. Admitting our shared incompetence was a bonding experience.

My in-laws and their husbands, who disagreed about everything from what color to paint their kitchen to where their children should go to college, did nothing without the other's consent. The wives relied on the husbands for the family's income, and the husbands depended on the wives for child-rearing. The women in Chuck's family were utterly unlike Natalia Ginzburg—who joined the Communist Party and was elected to Parliament as an independent left-wing deputy—but their marriages were strikingly similar. Every disagreement was a battle about whose decision ruled, who would be forced to defer, and who needed the other more. They told their stories about their husbands with great animation and a bitter kind of relish, trying to outdo one another. They were aggravated and energized by their quotidian skirmishes. Listening to them was like watching a murder mystery on TV. I was fascinated by the myriad details of marital discord, the small, missed cues that led to disastrous misunderstandings, and the plot twists that brought about the resolution. Human conflict is invigorating to witness from a distance. For my own life, though, I needed peace and quiet, a safe perch from which to observe the dramatic events going on elsewhere. I couldn't imagine sharing a house with a human companion I had to fight daily to renegotiate the balance of power.

Our town was the kind of place where everyone asked, "When are you going to start a family?" when a married couple remained childless into their thirties. Especially after Chuck and I bought a two-bedroom, Cape-Cod style house with a backyard half the size of a football field, no one believed us when we said we didn't plan to have kids.

"I spend the whole day with other people's children," Chuck, an elementary school teacher, said. "I don't have to raise my own."

But then I would admit to our friends, "I'm the one who doesn't want kids. I'm uncomfortable with young children. I can't imagine doing Chuck's job, much less being a mother."

I couldn't have been more explicit, but most people thought I was foregoing motherhood to concentrate on my career. Only a few women, themselves childless, understood that human babies didn't appeal to me. They laughed with sympathy when I said, "When I look at babies, I just think, *why can't they be furry?* I don't get why people make such a fuss over them."

Friends and neighbors often dropped by unannounced with their children in tow, and the adults stood around while the toddlers ran screaming through our house. It seemed unfair that I couldn't bring Dorian to their houses in return. But Dorian didn't have the temperament for a public life, so I trained him to wear a harness and a leash and accompany me to the backyard. At least he was out in public, in his own way. Dorian fell asleep in my lap while I read under the maple tree. He followed me from row to row as I weeded the vegetable garden, his leash looped around my ankle. I didn't let him roam around unrestrained because I imagined that something could capture his attention and that he could get confused, run in the wrong direction, and be lost forever.

One afternoon, I left him in the yard with his leash tied around a tree while I went inside to take a telephone call. What I thought would be a five-minute conversation stretched to nearly an hour. When I came back outside, Dorian was straining at the end of the leash, his whole body pointed toward the house. He must have been meowing for some time. His voice sounded hoarse.

I didn't leave him in the yard ever again, but Dorian now understood that I could abandon him outdoors just like I did inside. He still enjoyed sitting in the yard with me, but he was eager to get back in the house the moment I started gathering my things. We'd begin walking back across the yard, and he'd strain at the leash to make me move faster. If my arms were loaded with books or gardening tools, I worried about falling and not being able to catch myself, so I would unclip his leash and let him continue unrestrained ahead of me. Even I could see that he wasn't going anywhere without me.

I held open the door and said, "After you." He trotted into the kitchen and waited for me to get him out of the harness.

Dorian had no concept of the rest of the world and what I did in it and no desire to explore an unfamiliar place all by himself. I was the one who needed to be tied down and secured, through Dorian, to our home. Without him, I was adrift, a balloon cut off from its string, a fragile skin filled with nothing. I should have known all along: the leash and the harness were for me.

Chapter Six

Peach Boy

After living in Green Bay for six years, I received a summer grant to spend eight weeks in Japan and work on my second novel. I hadn't seen my maternal grandmother since the weekend I had said goodbye to her, my grandfather, and uncles thirteen years prior, but I was only going to visit her for two days because my mother had trained me from an early age not to be a burden on other people. My grandfather had died from a stroke two years after I left the country. Now, at ninety-five, my grandmother was living alone in their old house in a remote village without hotels or inns nearby, and even if there had been other accommodations, she would have been insulted if I hadn't stayed with her. Being able to host me was a point of pride with her.

Almost every hour I was there, she asked if she could fix me something to eat. She worried that I was too thin, I could get sick, I could die young. I should have humored her by eating all the food she offered me; instead, I left the house to take several long walks to get away from her nagging. As a child, I had run away from the table in tears whenever she heaped rice into my bowl and warned me about the seven gods inside every grain that I let go to waste. Nothing had changed in the decades since. I could only respond to her love by fleeing from it.

My Uncle Shiro, who joined us for a reunion dinner with another uncle, Yasuo, and his family, told me that everyone in our family was cursed with a powerful one-track mind. My grandmother, who had struggled to feed her family during the war, couldn't stop worrying about food. None of her children had inherited this concern, but my Aunt Keiko, who gave up her dream of becoming a pianist in order to marry and raise a family, joined a cult group after her children left home for college. You could often find her standing in front of the train station, preaching through a megaphone and passing out religious tracts. Even my mother's suicide—according to Uncle Shiro—was caused by her tenacious one-track mind latching onto the wrong thought: she had decided her life was worthless, and it was all she could think about, day after day, until she killed herself.

"But there's hope," he said. "You can choose something positive for your one-track mind to pursue. For me, it's my work. Your Uncle Kenichi has chosen the same thing. If your mother hadn't helped us with our tuition by going to work as a secretary, we wouldn't have been able to finish our education, so working hard at our jobs has also been our way of honoring her."

Shiro became a microbiology professor at a national university; Kenichi taught high school chemistry. They came from a wealthy family that had been reduced to poverty after the Second World War, when all the landowners were required to give up most of their property so the government could redistribute it among their tenant farmers.

"You can use your one-track mind to pursue your writing," Shiro told me.

Uncle Shiro probably would have never understood that my one-track mind was actually more obsessed with Dorian than it ever was with my writing. Dorian and I hadn't been apart for more than a few days at a stretch. Spending eight weeks away from him, an ocean away, was making me miserable—I'd call home just to hear Chuck say that Dorian was sleeping or eating or sitting in the sun—but at the time, I was too embarrassed to admit it, even to myself.

I now know that having a one-track mind isn't a special family curse but a common human trait. Everyone should have a harmless preoccupation to channel their obsessive tendencies, and what could be better than pet-keeping to prevent us from trying in vain to control everything and everyone around us? Pets are like portable oxygen tanks. Unless you are afraid of dogs or believe cats to be selfish and evil, petting them will lower your heart rate and blood pressure.

Animal companions give us something no human could or should: absolute mutual devotion. Since a pet's entire existence is dedicated to being with us, we don't have to hold back, give them space, or train them not to need us. We can indulge in a codependent relationship with impunity. Many of the stories my mother told me or read to me were about humans who were helped, or even saved, by animals.

One of them featured Momo Taro—Peach Boy—who was born from a giant peach that came floating down the river, where an old woman was washing clothes as her husband was gathering firewood in a nearby forest. The old woman took the peach home and cut it open. Momo Taro—a fully formed child—sprang out and was adopted by the childless couple who had been praying for a son. Eventually, Momo Taro grew up and went on an adventure. With the help of a dog, a monkey, and a pheasant, he sailed to a remote island and defeated the ogres who were living there, then brought back the treasures the ogres had stolen from the villagers on the mainland. The story didn't say what each animal did to help in the battle; the point of it was that their loyalty, not their skills, had led to Momo Taro's victory.

On the cover of the picture book my mother read to me, Momo Taro guarded the helm of a wooden ship in a samurai warrior's armor and helmet, pointing his sword toward the island of the ogres. The dog and the monkey stood beside him, one on each side, dressed in their matching indigo-dyed kimonos—the standard uniform of noblemen's servants. The pheasant, with its red head and rainbow-colored feathers, perched on top of the flagpole that flew a banner featuring a giant peach where the red disk symbolizing "the land of the rising sun" is normally centered on Japan's national flag. Bright orange rays emanated from the fruit, proclaiming Momo Taro's glory.

Momo Taro first encountered the dog, the monkey, and the pheasant when he was walking down the road with his mother's millet dumplings tucked into his waistband. The animals suddenly appeared before him and asked for a dumpling. Momo Taro gave one to each, and all three animals volunteered to fight alongside him on the island of the ogres.

When my mother read the story to me, I thought Momo Taro was lucky. If his dumplings hadn't been made of millet, the pheasant might not have had anything to eat. Everyone knows that birds are picky eaters.

My Uncle Yasuo, the only one of my three uncles to settle in the countryside near my grandparents, cooked his own suet cakes with seeds and berries to attract finches and warblers, and he was always trying to improve his recipe. He had more birds in his yard than all of his neighbors combined. Millet was in Yasuo's suet cakes and also in the mix that my piano teacher fed to her canary, so I figured a dumpling made of millet had a good chance of appealing to a pheasant.

The Momo Taro legend, a story known to every schoolchild, started in Okayama, a city famous for its peach orchards. On an elementary school field trip during peach season, my classmates and I bought millet dumplings there as a souvenir. Pale green, sticky, and extremely sweet, they were packed in a wooden box whose front had a picture of Momo Taro and his companions walking down a dusty country road. The dumplings stuck to my teeth like sugary glue, but I kept eating them because I believed them to be magical and legendary. On the bus ride home, we learned Momo Taro's song about each of the animals begging for dumplings. One group sang Momo Taro's part while the other group sang the parts belonging to each of the animals. There were no Momo Taro songs about killing ogres or being born from a peach, so I surmised that sharing his dumplings with the animals was Momo Taro's most heroic deed. Only a hero could turn wild animals into faithful servants by offering them the perfect food.

Originally, the story might have been about piety (how the old couple's prayers were answered) or even nationalism (how a hero from the mainland vanquished the ogres on a remote island). But I think it's a parable about the importance of animal companions. The dog, the monkey, and the pheasant are representatives of three distinct groups inside the animal kingdom: four-legged mammals, primates like us, and birds in the sky. To become a hero, Momo Taro, a boy born from a peach, needed all three by his side. Humans can only prosper with help from the creatures who share the world with us.

Cat and Bird

A woman I met in Wisconsin had a pet turkey named "Christmas," one of the two birds that had been raised by her brother-in-law for the holiday table. After he'd butchered the first turkey—"Thanksgiving"—outside the birds' pen, though, Christmas took to running around, squawking and flapping his wings in distress every time my friend's brother-in-law approached the barn.

He finally brought Christmas to stay with his sister-in-law, who was a vegetarian.

"He goes nuts," the man said. "I can't stand having him around."

Christmas had to be confined to his pen at night to stay safe from foxes and coyotes, but my friend and her husband let him roam around the yard during the day. He'd follow them and eat corn out of their hands. One day, the husband fell off a ladder and broke his leg; Christmas stood over him squawking so loudly that my friend heard him from inside the house.

"If that bird hadn't alerted me," she said, "my husband could have laid there for hours while I was going about my business, totally unaware."

People generally assume that turkeys are dumb. I'm not sure if Christmas was smart enough to realize that not all humans meant to harm him or stupid enough not to understand that other humans were capable of the same act. He correctly deduced that my friend's brother-in-law was planning to kill him and that her husband was hurt by his fall, but what do injury, life, and death mean to a bird? What matters in this scenario isn't the turkey's level of intelligence but the human's.

The story of Christmas is the real-life version of my mother's bedtime stories. But in the fairy tales she told me repeatedly, the animals were always smarter and kinder than the humans. They gave back much more than they owed, rewarding the humans with great bravery, wealth, or status in return for a minor act of kindness, such as offering a millet cake or putting out a handful of seeds on a cold day or releasing the animal from a trap at no risk to themselves.

"Puss in Boots," which was first published by Charles Perrault in 1697, was another of her favorites. In that story, the miller's youngest son was disappointed when his father died and left him nothing but a cat. He thought the only useful thing you could do with a cat might be to eat it. The boy decided to spare its life and agreed to look for the pair of boots and the sack that the cat requested, mostly because he had no idea what else to do. The cat turned out to be his faithful servant, life coach, and best friend rolled into one. The boy married a princess while his older brothers, who had inherited their father's property, remained in their humble stations in life.

As a child, I loved this story but didn't understand its moral. The right footwear can transform an ordinary barn cat into a magical being? It's okay to exaggerate and even lie to help a friend? If a cat tells you to take off your clothes and jump into a river, you should just do it? My mother was not a storyteller who hit you over the head with a lesson. The real fun was in speculating together about all the possible interpretations, why the characters acted the way they did, or how the story might have turned out differently. After decades of living with cats and hearing other people's pet stories, though, I finally get it. "Puss in Boots" is about the wisdom of recognizing an animal as a companion rather than as a resource to be exploited. It's shortsighted to eat the cat. Befriending him—or letting him befriend you—is the smarter move.

Cat and Bird

Like the love of music or the appreciation for color, the desire for animal companionship may be a universal human longing, but some people, even people within the same family, feel it more than others. Of my grandmother's six children, my mother was the only one who ever kept a pet or put breadcrumbs on the balcony for house sparrows, the plainest, commonest birds. Yasuo, who attracted rare finches and warblers to his yard, was an outdoorsman. As a teenager, he used to skip school and spend the day in the woods, catching songbirds to keep or sell as caged pets. According to Uncle Kenichi, who accompanied him once or twice, Yasuo could imitate several birdsongs to lure the animals into the mist nets he set.

"He sat in the cold for hours," Kenichi said, "just waiting for birds. I didn't have the patience to do that."

As an adult, Yasuo knew when certain freshwater fish were migrating through the river near my grandparents' house and which of the wild persimmon trees on the mountain paths bore sweet fruit instead of tart. If Yasuo had lived in Wisconsin, he would have hunted wild turkeys or deer for Thanksgiving: he was a modern-day hunter-gatherer. He teased me for being too squeamish to gut the fish he caught, still alive in a pail of water, and he chided my mother for allowing me to become too sentimental about nature.

My mother was delighted by the house sparrows, especially in the spring when they brought their babies and fed them beak to beak. She claimed she could tell the frequent visitors apart by their behavior: the bossy birds chased the others away, though the shy but clever ones would return when the bossy ones were fighting, steal a small crumb, and fly away. To her, the sparrows on our balcony were nearly human, like characters in a story. That's how she talked about Neko-chan, too, years after he went missing. In the story she told and retold, he was the guardian of my infancy, the symbol of my independent nature, a magical being who protected me in her absence. My brother and I were like the children in Perrault's fable. Jumpei was destined to inherit our family's material possessions, but our mother left me the legendary cat, the love of animals, and the stories to sustain me for life.

Chapter Seven

Dorian

The winter Dorian was seven years old, field mice moved into our basement and crawled up to the kitchen to forage in the middle of the night. They refused to leave even after we installed a gadget that made disturbing noises only they could hear. Chuck and I put away all our food into sealed containers, but the mice chewed through the plastic lid of our coffee can and ate the grounds. So I didn't feel so bad when Dorian left dead mice on the floor beside the bed, lightly nibbled on the head or the tail but otherwise intact, as if he'd become my professional food taster to make sure they were safe for me to eat. As he watched me throw the carcasses into the yard for the crows and other scavengers, it's possible he thought I wanted fresher food. Soon he started bringing me mice that were still alive.

When Dorian came running up the stairs with a live mouse in his mouth, there was no mistaking what was going on. The mouse would be making a terrible squeaking noise, and Dorian would half-huff and half-grunt with his mouth full. It wasn't as though either Chuck or I could sleep through this event. We'd both sit bolt upright, and I'd turn on my bedside lamp.

"He's your cat," Chuck would say as he lay back down and covered his head with a pillow.

I responded by sleeping with a stack of brown lunch bags, a whisk broom, and a dustpan so I could catch the mice, put them in the bag, and release them outside.

Dorian never dropped any mouse, dead or alive, on Chuck's side of the bed. He deposited mice on my pillow, in my shoes, and, once, into a gym bag that I hadn't been able to close because my tennis racket was sticking out of it. Chuck left his shoes and book bags lying around too, but Dorian ignored his belongings completely.

The most widely accepted theory about why cats bring us their catch is that they are trying to teach us how to hunt. If this is true, then Dorian and I were experiencing a rare role reversal. He was acting like a mother cat who brings back a maimed mouse and lets her kittens finish it off, just as I had become adept with the whisk broom, dustpan, and bag. Dorian would follow me as I padded down the stairs in my pajamas and wait by the door while I put on my boots, walked across the yard, upended the bag under the maple trees, and trekked back to the house. Apparently satisfied with my work, he would either come back to bed or resume the hunt.

I never would have married a man with a big, dramatic personality, and yet I was simultaneously mortified and thrilled by Dorian's aggression toward every human he met besides me.

"My cat is terrible," I said, feeling a bit of pride as well as irritation when Dorian hissed, pounced, bit, and drew blood. I found it hilarious that our veterinarian, Dr. Nyren, who was in his sixties and also took care of my mother-in-law's two felines, told her that Dorian was the absolute worst cat he had ever doctored.

"He must have handled hundreds, maybe even thousands of cats, and he considers Dorian to be a true terror," I bragged to my friends.

On his first visit, Dorian whirled around like a dervish and opened a sizable gash on Dr. Nyren's arm. After that, the doctor would meet us in the waiting room, accompanied by the sole male tech at the clinic, a young man who was easily over six feet tall. The technician wore long leather gloves up to his elbows. Dr. Nyren didn't want me hovering over them while they gave Dorian his annual physical exam and booster shots. They'd take him to the back room inside his blue plastic pet carrier and return him to me still (or again) inside the carrier. The difference between the before and after was in the volume and pitch of the growls emanating from within. Because Dorian didn't sit still when he was upset, the whole carrier, placed on the floor, rocked from side to side while I stood at the counter trying to pay for the visit. I then understood why people in the Middle Ages thought cats were possessed by demons.

No matter what I had to do to take care of him, Dorian never bit or scratched me. With me, he was always a model patient, but that was his choice. It was never about me being "good with animals" or him being genuinely submissive. I controlled all the major aspects of his life, but that wasn't enough. Every day with him was an all-out war for supremacy. I took it personally when he ate a half-moon shape out of the cuff of my favorite angora sweater when I left it draped over my suitcase. He abhorred that suitcase and everything that went into it.

I complained when he woke me up in the middle of the night (once, by knocking my coffee cups off the mug tree and breaking all of them) or when he sat on the book I was trying to read, but I felt hurt if I wanted to take a break from my writing and he was sleeping. "Hey," I'd whisper loudly into his ear, "I need some attention now." Then I'd pluck him off the couch where he was sound asleep and hold him upside down by his hind legs and swing him back and forth or sling him over my shoulder like a sack of potatoes and carry him around the house until he woke up.

Cat and Bird

The basement office where Dorian watched over my writing had one window high up on the wall. Snow covered it completely in the winter; even in the summer, all I could see was grass poking through the ground above my head. After my first book was published, I decided to find a place, a room of my own, to write in.

I rented an apartment on a downtown block that had been destroyed by a fire in 1882 and rebuilt. Because all the "new" construction was designed in the same Italianate style, the buildings' facades blended seamlessly one to the next. My little apartment, which was upstairs from a photography studio, overlooked the only busy thoroughfare in town, and the buildings across the street were mirror images of ours. It had two small bedrooms, a galley kitchen, and a closet-sized bathroom. I put my desk in front of the wall of exposed bricks that formed slightly crooked horizontal lines, their colors varying from rust to salmon to cream. The bricks fit together without being identical, like long sentences and short sentences blending into a paragraph. Dorian and I drove there on the days I wrote. The desk, the couch I bought for Dorian, and a dozen milk cartons full of old stories, notes, and books, were all he and I needed in our writing sanctuary. Gradually, I added kitchen utensils, more books, and supplies for my knitting and weaving.

When I decided to leave my marriage, the writing studio was the logical place for Dorian and me to move into. I liked the idea of writing and living in the same space. Dorian and I slept on the floor among boxes of writing notes and yarn. Finally, I thought, my life would be as seamless as the old bricks in the neighborhood from a bygone era. Every morning I woke up to the sound of traffic, which gave the illusion of living in a metropolis. The quaint apartment was the most unlikely place for a woman from Japan to end up. A childless, divorced foreigner nearing forty, I was a misfit through and through. The majority of women around me were raising children of their own or getting ready to be grandmothers. Still, unlike in Japan—where my childlessness and divorce would have disgraced my entire family—no one in Green Bay expected anything from me. I would never be understood or accepted, but I was free to do as I pleased.

I had told Chuck I might look for another job in a larger city. All I asked for in the divorce settlement was my half of the principle we had paid off on the mortgage at the time of my departure, which could be given to me in the future if I ever needed it. Because we'd owned the house for ten years, the amount would have been enough for a down payment on a new home. I considered buying a condominium in Milwaukee, 120 miles south. I could commute to my job by keeping the studio to stay in during the week. But the thought of all that driving exhausted me. Dorian was a superb car traveler, but he was now fifteen years old. Carting him between two cities every week—or for that matter, finding another job and moving us to an entirely new place—became less and less practical as time passed.

I knew I couldn't spend the rest of my life in that tiny studio. But I couldn't imagine Dorian and me relocating, even after I started dating a colleague, Peter, who was also newly divorced, and he asked me to move in with him and his three cats. Dorian hadn't seen another cat since he'd been at his breeder's. There was no way he could adjust to being one of four cats sharing a house. Besides, he hissed and growled at Peter every time they met. So Dorian and I sank deeper into our

Cat and Bird

apartment's protective time warp, where I could tend to him and my other essentials: writing, running, and the friends I had made over the years, including the volunteers I had met through bird rescue. They were locals who could blend into the crowd, but they were also oddballs: never married or married many times and divorced, childless or estranged from their children, more comfortable with animals than with people. We were like the miscellaneous birds that fell out of their nests and ended up inside laundry baskets in our spare bedrooms. Although most of us no longer had time to volunteer at the sanctuary, we continued to meet up for meals, movies, and nature walks.

Apart from this group, my closest friend in town was Jim, a priest and art teacher who made sculptures from old books. The obsessive attention he brought to his work, sculpting books to open up like flowers by crinkling every page by hand, was something the two of us—and not many others, even among our group of friends—could understand.

Jim's mother had died from cancer when he was in college, and by the time we became friends in our early thirties, he was no longer in touch with his father. We traipsed through the overgrown fields of the abbey where he lived, cutting Queen Anne's lace, chicory, and pampas grass that he would arrange into three-foot-tall altar decorations held together by wire. He had studied ikebana, the art of Japanese flower arrangement, which I finally understood was a form of sculpture rather than a prissy hobby among genteel Japanese women who had nothing better to do. He knew how hard it was to make art look easy.

Fortunately, my lack of religious faith never came between us. "I believe in beauty," Jim said.

My conversations with him kept me from giving up on the book I had traveled to Japan to write. Writing was supposed to be a quiet, purposeful activity, but sometimes it wasn't quiet at all. More often than not, it was an internal cacophony of contradictory messages shouting and mumbling in a hundred obstructionist waves of recognition, like hundreds of birds declaring their territory inside my head. But once in a while, the noise would die down and leave me with a single distinct bird call, a truth that I was finally eager to accept and compress into written words.

In Japan, I had asked my uncles and my grandmother about their experiences during the Second World War. I thought that hearing those stories would inspire me to write a historical novel. But once I was back in Green Bay, sitting at my desk in front of the nineteenth-century brick wall, I couldn't even begin to imagine my grandmother as a young mother in wartime Japan. During my eight weeks there, I had traveled around the country, reconnected with my school friends, and found my way around my hometown again. I even thought I might return periodically in the future. But then, as soon as I got on the plane, I was so relieved to be leaving that by the time we were in the air, I couldn't believe I had entertained, even for a moment, the idea of coming back. Unlike the birds who traveled thousands of miles every year, I could not migrate between countries.

My grandmother died the following year. My uncles and I only exchanged a few brief letters afterward, and I understood that the true story was that of my estrangement, a story I could tell only in a memoir. But I decided to write a young adult novel first about a Japanese girl who finds solace in the birds she encounters in the mountains near her home.

Every summer of my childhood, I heard the songbirds my uncle attracted to his yard with the special food he made, but I had no idea if they were year-round residents or summer visitors.

Cat and Bird

Birds migrate between north and south, not east and west; only a few common species, like house sparrows and crows, are seen all over the world. I bought a field guide to the birds of Japan and compiled a list of migratory birds that nested in the mountains near Kobe. Then I took a day trip to the Field Museum in Chicago, where the curator brought out a dozen specimens from their international ornithological collection and left me to study them on my own.

The bush warbler, an olive-green bird the size of my index finger, still had its original tag tied around its leg with a single white thread. The Japanese script, in blue ink that reminded me of the fountain pen my maternal grandfather had used to write in his diary, identified its provenance: "Misaki Peninsula, May 1925." My mother was born in February 1928 and died in March 1969. Her whole life had come and gone in the time this bird had spent in a museum drawer.

The bush warbler and the thread of words he carried connected me to the mountains of my childhood, but I could only travel there in my writing from the safety of my temporary shelter, an apartment that was a time capsule of someone else's history. Dorian fortified my solitude while I tried to accept another truth: I couldn't escape my mother's fate without losing her family.

In spite of his horrendous behavior, Dorian always had excellent physicals. He was a hardy cat; he seldom threw up hairballs or undigested food. So I knew something was wrong when he wasn't finishing his food. School was out for the summer and I was home all day with him. One hot day, I noticed him breathing with his mouth open and took him to Dr. Nyren immediately. His behavior was the same as usual—he started spitting and hissing the minute we entered the building—but after the physical, I had to leave him for tests. When I picked him up a few hours later, he was quiet inside the carrier; the anesthesia he'd been given had made him groggy. The X-rays and biopsy confirmed that he had a malignant tumor on his lung. No treatment was available, just palliative care. Since he wasn't expected to live long enough to suffer the long-term side effects, he could be given high doses of steroids to ease his breathing and increase his appetite.

Dorian had no trouble swallowing the pills I crammed into his mouth, and the medication was amazingly effective. Within days, he was breathing normally and eating his food again. He jumped into my lap, purred loudly when I petted him, and followed me around the apartment instead of slumping back to sleep. Even so, I knew that in a few weeks or months, the cancer would spread and the steroids would ravage the rest of his body.

After his grandmother's death from cancer, Chuck said he would rather die than subject himself to useless treatments.

I wouldn't want to linger either, just waiting to die, though I was more worried about the thoughts inside my head than what might happen to my body. If I knew I had only a few weeks to live, I would spend every waking moment pondering my fate—the eternal torment of hell or the total extinction of nonbeing. I might even succumb to the temptation of a deathbed conversion.

Of course, Dorian wouldn't spend sleepless nights becoming too paralyzed to enjoy the last good stretch while it lasted. So I decided it was okay not to hasten the end, but I agonized over the decision. I worried that I might be holding on to him more for my sake than his.

Cat and Bird

Chuck and I had been divorced for two years by then, but we still played tennis every week and had coffee afterward at a nearby café. Whenever I went out of town, Dorian would stay at our old house with Chuck, the only other person who could take care of him. I knew they both enjoyed these reunions, so after I told Chuck about Dorian's prognosis, I asked him if he wanted to have coffee in my apartment and visit Dorian.

"No," Chuck said. "I'd rather remember him when he was really himself."

I assured him that Dorian was still looking and feeling pretty normal. He had lost some weight at the start of his illness and hadn't gained it back—he never would—but otherwise, he was the same cat Chuck had known all along.

"It's okay," he said. "Really, I don't have to see him now."

Chuck hadn't visited his grandparents when they were dying because he considered it artificial to "say goodbye" if a person could no longer fully respond. When his grandfather was in the emergency room with a brain aneurysm and his father called to say that he wasn't expected to live through the night, Chuck said, "I'd rather remember when he was really himself."

So when I called Chuck several weeks later to say I was taking Dorian to the vet for the last time and asked if he wanted to go with me, I wasn't surprised when he said again he preferred to remember Dorian healthy. I personally believe that the death of someone you love will always seem unfair, untimely, and unreal, so boycotting the last goodbye is a useless attempt to delude yourself into thinking you have some control over the situation. Still, in keeping with our worldview, whatever way Chuck chose to face Dorian's death was his business. I just didn't want to spend the last twenty minutes of Dorian's life with me behind the wheel and him in the pet carrier. I wanted to be in the passenger's seat with him in my lap.

But all I could say was, "I understand."

I couldn't stand having people help me against their will. If Chuck didn't want to be there for me, then I didn't want him around. I'd been worried about letting Dorian die too soon or too late. It was possible that my idea about what was right for him had been utterly wrong. That was the heartbreak of the situation. For nearly eighteen years, I could assume—or harmlessly delude myself into thinking—that Dorian's needs and my needs were the same: a comfortable home, quiet days and evenings together, play, eat, sleep, repeat. Once he started dying, though, his physical comfort was the only thing that mattered. My own feelings—and my desire for him to be with me forever—were eliminated from the equation. Our paths had diverged even while he was still alive.

As it turned out, the decisions I made for Dorian were as right as such decisions could be. I delayed the end while the medication was working and he was feeling well enough. I noticed and acted right away when his condition began to deteriorate. I had asked the veterinarian for a tranquilizer to give him at home so Dorian wouldn't gather what little strength he had left to make the procedure even worse. I knew when he was in my lap and I was giving him the pill that we were saying goodbye in the least horrible way possible. We sat together for thirty minutes, waiting for the medication to start working, and then I took him to the vet and held him until the end without falling apart.

The wrong decision I made was about Chuck. I had no right to assume he didn't want to help me. I only asked him on the phone, "Do you want to come with me?" presenting it as something he could do or not do for himself, not for me. I should have said, "I know this isn't something you want to do, but I need you to drive so I can hold Dorian and give him all of my attention before I have to let him go. Will you help me?" He had never before accompanied Dorian and me to the vet. It would have been awkward and painful for him to go with us just this once. I would have been asking for the impossible, really. Still, if I had asked and he had said no, we would have both had the satisfaction of being honest.

"I promise to tell you the hard truths," one of my friends in Boston declared in her wedding vows. Chuck and I hadn't made personalized vows—we just repeated what the judge had told us to say once we made sure the vows didn't require me to "obey"— but if we had written ours, they would have started and ended with a promise to respect our continued autonomy, to allow each of us to discover the hard truths for ourselves.

After Dorian died, my friends sent me cards, but they found it difficult to say something nice about him. They didn't want to lie, so they wrote, "We know he meant so much to you," "You and he were so close," "You must miss him very much," and— best of all—"You've had him for so long," as though Dorian had overstayed his welcome on the planet. Not one person could say, in writing or in person, "He was a great cat," or "We'll miss him too." Dorian had terrorized and alienated all of my friends, and yet they knew how much I loved him and needed to be consoled. Their strained effort made me laugh and cry at once.

One of my friends let me bury Dorian in his backyard, even though Dorian had bitten him multiple times. Years later, before he got married and moved to another house, my friend told the new owners about the grave so it would not be disturbed. Jim, who knew the new owners as his parishioners, visited the grave and called me from there.

"The grave looks very secure," he said. "The trees around it have grown quite a bit."

I could still picture the gray rock I had found at Lake Michigan to mark the spot.

Dorian died two months short of his eighteenth birthday. I went to stay with Peter for a few days afterward, but all I did was cry. When I was halfway coherent, I explained that missing Dorian also meant missing the person I used to be with him. His death was a thousand times more devastating than my divorce, after which I was still myself. I didn't even lose Chuck, really, since we regularly played tennis and had coffee.

Trying to cheer me up, Peter took me to my favorite restaurant, but as we were crossing the road in front of the building, I said, "If a big truck came and hit me now, it would be no loss."

Peter and I stopped walking. The restaurant was on the edge of town, in a lot surrounded by trees. There was no vehicle in sight, just the empty road stretching in both directions. Finally, he said, "Maybe you should get another cat, a cat of your own."

Perhaps he meant that if I lived with him and his cats, I could still get a cat trained to bond only with me, but I didn't ask him. To me, getting my own cat meant only one thing: just the two of us, the cat and me, alone, together.

No matter how many cats I had in the future, there would never be another Dorian, which meant that nothing would ever be the way it was. My whole existence, as I knew it, was over. Still, Peter was right. Like it or not, I only had two choices: give up and die or take a chance on a different life.

"If I get my own cat," I said. "I'll never move in with you. I probably wouldn't even stay at your house because I'd be too busy bonding with the kitten."

Peter didn't seem surprised. "That's okay," he said. "I just want you to be happy."

Although we kept dating a while longer, he was letting me go and, at the same time, giving himself a way out. He understood—perhaps he suspected all along—that I was never serious about us. Because everyone our age was married or trying to get remarried, I found it easier to be part of a couple. Peter was from another small town in Wisconsin, so being with him also conferred an indirect insider status that made me feel less conspicuous in Green Bay. Dorian had been my perfect reason for not moving in with him, but with Dorian gone, the thought of living with anyone else made me wish I would get run over by a truck.

I'd rather die, I was saying to myself and to Peter, than give up my solitude. I wasn't rejecting him personally. I was tired of pretending I believed in the importance of romance and marriage. Single, married, or divorced, I was who I was by myself. My mother had killed herself because she believed she was nothing without a husband who loved her. Every night of our last year together, I had promised her that I would find meaning in the life I made on my own.

Dorian had helped me keep my promise to my mother by watching over my writing and protecting my solitude even while I was married to Chuck. His fierce devotion to me had saved me from repeating the same unhappy marriage I had left. And so, in his honor, I would start the second half of my life by finding another feline companion to inherit his guardianship.

Chapter Eight

Oscar

The regional cat show where I met Oscar for the first time was held in a high school gymnasium in a small town south of Milwaukee. Peter and I left Green Bay early in the morning and drove nonstop. Neither of us had ever attended a cat show before, but I wasn't in the mood to look around when we got there. Among the rows of fold-out tables displaying cats and kittens, cat toys and furniture, and cat-themed clothes and accessories for humans, I found the Siamese cat breeder I had talked to on the phone.

The four kittens she had available sat in a tangle of paws and tails inside a mesh carrier that resembled a tent. Their enormous ears reminded me of deformed tulip buds. Three were dozing off. I pointed to the one kitten whose eyes were open and said, "That one." He regarded me, I thought, with skepticism, but it was too late. The breeder, a retired nurse in a beige pantsuit, scooped him out of the tent and into the blue plastic carrier that had once been Dorian's. I handed over my check and picked up the carrier, which felt astonishingly light. The kitten had settled himself in the back corner, curled up on an old T-shirt. Without seeing the rest of the show, Peter and I headed back to the freeway. Three hours later, he dropped Oscar and me off at my apartment and drove away so the kitten would understand from the beginning that I was the only important person in his life. I named him after Oscar Wilde, a nod to Dorian's legacy.

After sleeping through the entire car ride, the new kitten was wide awake and leery of me. The T-shirt, which was supposed to acclimate him to my scent, hadn't worked. He spent the first night crouched in the corner of my bedroom. Every time I woke up, he was staring at me from among a pile of shoes in the corner. Because the room was small, he was only ever about five feet away, but his whole posture exuded wariness. Having a cat who considered me a threat to his safety was worse than being alone. If he was going to snub me, I thought, he should hide in the other room. At twelve weeks old, the kitten was smaller than my size seven sneakers. His fur was so pale that it was almost white. He might disappear, never to be seen again, like the hamsters Chuck kept losing in his classroom.

At dawn, I opened my eyes just in time to see the kitten emerge from his hiding place and climb onto my futon. I sat up, cross-legged, in my pajamas. Oscar circled me, rubbing his forehead against my hands and knees, my ankles and feet, my pajama legs, my back, and my face and hair when I leaned into him. He arched his back and purred loudly when I petted him. No rescue party had arrived during the night to take him back to his mother, brothers, and original caretaker. It was me or nobody. He rolled on the futon and offered me his stomach to scratch. Then he walked around the room, bumping into the dresser and the lampstand, rubbing his head on the carpet and the walls, returning to my side every few minutes to headbutt me and flop down to be petted. After I'd given him enough attention, he jumped up to resume his investigation, venturing out into other parts of the apartment and coming back for more headbutts and stomach scratches.

Cats have a scent gland under the skin of their forehead, which they can activate by rubbing. Oscar was staking out his new home by leaving his scent on the furniture, the carpet, and the walls and then returning to mark me too. He now owned everything he touched and me most of all.

I still cried about Dorian, but the apartment was a different place with a kitten dashing from room to room and jumping from the floor to my shoulder to cling to my neck. Oscar was all about movement. Watching him sprint around, nearly crashing into the walls, I wondered if I too should find a larger life. So when a writing center in Minnesota offered me a teaching residency for the following summer, I accepted, though I said I would have to bring Oscar.

Oscar meowed nonstop during the six-hour drive but calmed down when I carried him into the new apartment in downtown Minneapolis. He waited for me to finish unloading the car, then pranced out eagerly the moment I opened the carrier. As I unpacked my clothes and books, he rubbed his head on the furniture in every room and periodically checked in with me for a brief petting session. He finally settled on the couch to take a nap. Even though the apartment was twice the size of ours in Green Bay, with furniture utterly unlike anything I owned, Oscar understood the couch was where we would sit down to read and nap during the day, the bed was where we'd sleep at night, his food and water bowls were in the kitchen, and his litter box was in the bathroom. In just half an hour, he had connected the dots and mapped out his universe.

Without Oscar, I would have driven back from class every evening and gone straight to bed instead of running around the apartment playing with him, drinking coffee at midnight, and settling on the couch to read so we could fall asleep twice every night: first dozing off on the couch, then getting up a few hours later and officially going to bed—a routine that's as cozy with a cat as it is pitiful alone. I acclimated to Minneapolis-St. Paul the way Oscar had surveyed the apartment. On foot, on my bike, in my car, I'd venture out, explore a small area, and circle back.

Cat and Bird

My mental map of the Twin Cities had Oscar at its center. Only seven pounds fully grown, he was so light on his feet that he could greet me by jumping straight off the floor to my shoulder. As I put my bike or my groceries away, he'd reposition himself to face forward. His brown tail, which was longer than the rest of his body, would wrap around the back of my neck and dangle down my shoulder. We'd walk around the whole apartment so he could get a human's-eye view.

Minneapolis in 1998 was far from racially diverse—I seldom saw other Asian people or people of any color except white—but whether I was visiting museums, shopping for groceries, or walking around various neighborhoods, no one ever looked at me unless we were actually speaking to each other. For the first time in over a decade, I could go about my business without provoking curiosity or alarm. In Green Bay, I hadn't had the audacity to stare back, so I seldom noticed anyone's appearance or mannerisms. Now, observing humans on a city street was as easy as watching birds on a nature trail. I could eavesdrop on people's conversations or discreetly glance at their clothes and gestures. I could even strike up a casual conversation with a stranger in the grocery store without being treated like a cultural ambassador. Like any normal person, I could be seen and heard only when I chose to be.

When Oscar and I returned to Green Bay, I looked through the national job listings published annually by the Association of Writers and Writing Programs. None of the openings with a reasonable teaching load were in the midwestern cities I knew well, but I updated my vitae and sent out a dozen applications for jobs in large cities and college towns around the country. In November, I was stunned to be contacted for an on-campus interview at Harvard for a five-year lectureship to teach nonfiction writing. After a one-hour interview with five faculty members and no teaching demonstration or public presentation, I was offered the position by phone while I was waiting to board my flight home.

I had applied to the job in the same spirit in which people purchase lottery tickets. The idea of teaching at a university that never would have let me in as a student was absurd. And unlike the other jobs I had applied to, the post was only temporary. I had no concept of what I would do after the five-year contract was over. Since job postings changed from year to year, there was no guarantee the right opening would come up when I needed it next, and accepting the lectureship at Harvard would expose me to risk and uncertainty.

In the twenty-one years since I had left Japan, I had done everything I could to avoid change. I was still living two hundred miles from where I had first ended up in Illinois. I had a steady, undemanding job in an uneventful place, among people who dismissed me as a foreigner. I was safe, but only in the way that the bush warbler was safe inside the drawer at the Field Museum. For the last half century or more, I might have been the only person who saw and could decipher the writing on the provenance tag left around the bird's leg. The bush warbler had been a source of inspiration for my novel, but now its memory became a warning.

I was forty-one, the exact age my mother was when she killed herself. If I didn't leave Green Bay now by the hardest, most unlikely path, I would spend the rest of my life—the forty or more years my mother didn't get to live—paralyzed by a past that was long gone, holding on to words that no one would read. The isolation of Green Bay had protected me so far, allowing me to travel back to my childhood in my writing and recover some of the stories my mother had meant to pass on to me. But the past was beyond anyone's ability to preserve or restore. The life I had with my mother was gone forever, no matter how clearly I remembered it. Takako had wanted to protect me from her unhappiness, but she also longed for me to live as a strong and independent woman. To truly honor her legacy, I had to finally abandon my temporary shelter and face the risks I had been avoiding. Only then could the next forty years be an adventure that neither my mother nor I could have predicted on those evenings she cried and I tried in vain to console her.

I didn't take the lectureship on the spot, standing in line at the airport. But as soon as I got home, I called Harvard to accept the offer and withdrew my other applications. I gave up my tenure at the Catholic college without negotiating a return.

I traveled to Cambridge over spring break, where my realtor took me to a 440-square-foot condominium apartment on the top floor of a brownstone near Harvard Square. The tiny studio with the large windows overlooking a tree-lined street was perfect for Oscar and me. My mortgage would be less than the rent I would pay in the same neighborhood. I didn't have to explain, justify, or defend my decision to anyone before offering the entire asking price to expedite the sale. I only had to ascertain that the building allowed pets and that the living room window would be repaired to stay open without the stick that was currently holding it up—so Oscar could sit safely on the windowsill.

"Fix LR window so it will not fall on cat," the realtor scribbled on her notepad. If she thought I was foolish to be more concerned about Oscar's safety than about the lack of closet space or the cracks in the ceiling, she didn't let on.

I tried to acclimate Oscar to the 1,100-mile car ride we would have to undertake together, but driving half a mile to the nearest frozen custard stand was as tortuous for him as if we were traveling cross-country. He paced inside the carrier; he yowled and even hissed. During our last practice session—freeway driving—I made the mistake of letting him out of the carrier, which almost got us killed when he clung to my neck and made it impossible for me to look over my shoulder at the merging traffic. The driver of the milk truck that nearly hit us must have seen me trying to peel a tiny feline off my shoulder and stuff him back into the carrier, but he just leaned on his horn and sped off.

Oscar had huge ears like Yoda's and a creamy face with a dark chocolate smudge around the nose. He often greeted guests by climbing all over them, purring. He liked to perch on the crook of my elbow and take tiny sips of white wine from the glass I tilted toward him. Where Dorian had inspired fear in others and a perverse pride in me, Oscar made everyone smile and feel protective toward him. Dorian and I could have camped out in the car on the way to Massachusetts, but I couldn't subject Oscar to over twenty hours of driving without proper breaks in pet-friendly motels.

We started on our drive to Cambridge in May 1999. The moving van had already picked up my furniture and boxes, so all I had to load in the car were my suitcase, Oscar's food, his litter box and toys, the cooler of food I'd prepared for myself so I wouldn't have to stop and leave Oscar in the car, and a few boxes of bedding and kitchen utensils. Oscar yowled and paced, but we made it to Milwaukee, then to Chicago. But once I reached the tangle of highways south of Chicago, I knew we had entered unknown territory.

Whenever I had to glance at the road atlas propped open between the gear shift and the dashboard and then scan the highway signs coming up, I tossed a few treats into the carrier, knowing that Oscar couldn't chew and meow at the same time. He quieted down long enough to let me concentrate. In a motel room in Sandusky, Ohio, he slept soundly all night, only to growl as soon as we got back in the car. When the highway peeled away from Lake Erie outside Buffalo, separating us from the last of the Great Lakes, I was tempted to add my own wail of dismay at our dislocation. Finally, as we crossed the Charles River into Cambridge, I couldn't believe we had arrived without getting lost.

In our still-empty apartment, Oscar dashed out of the carrier and went immediately to work, claiming his new territory. The first night there, he crawled inside the sleeping bag I put on the floor and slept in my arms as he had always done. It would be days before our furniture arrived, but he didn't care. For Oscar, home was wherever we were living together. One city was the same as another. He couldn't wait to explore an unfamiliar place and turn it into a new home. And even though the move had been my idea, I came to think of him as my guide.

In my new neighborhood, I was never the only Asian woman on the street. Sometimes, all the people sitting inside the small café nearby had dark hair like mine. Walking through Harvard Square, I would overhear bits of conversation in Japanese as a small group of women in pastel-colored blouses and knit pants or straight skirts stepped out of a storefront, their faces lightly made up, and if one of them laughed, her hand immediately flew up to cover her mouth in a gesture of modesty while the others followed suit, their hands also fluttering up to their faces. I had to remind myself that these were not my mother and her friends finally free to enjoy a leisurely afternoon in public but most likely expatriate *okusan* ("honorable wives") whose husbands worked in the area, and I was now their age, a year older than Takako had ever been.

Around the corner from my apartment, an old Sears and Roebuck building had been converted into a Japanese mall with a grocery store, a cosmetic counter of Shiseido products, restaurants made up to resemble the ramshackle noodle stands near Japanese commuter train stations, and a bakery that sold squishy, melon-shaped loaves covered with sugar that sparkled like shards of glass. I knew, from the last one I had eaten at eight or nine, that the loaf was filled with artificially flavored bean paste. I had moved 1,100 miles farther from Japan to live a five-minute walk from the worst bread of my childhood. Henri—a classmate from graduate school and my only friend in Boston—left for Germany at the end of the summer. After that, I had no one but Oscar to whom I could explain why the Japanese mall scared me, how it made me imagine being sucked back into my past just as I was trying to figure out my future.

Our first summer in Cambridge ended with a trip to western Massachusetts. Oscar quickly checked out our room at the Howard Johnson's, rubbing his forehead on every surface and then on me, the guidepost at the center of his range. Having mastered his territory and confirmed the source of his food and water, he settled right in. I didn't know anyone in the area, so after sightseeing and birdwatching all day by myself, I'd return each night to have dinner with him in our hotel room. We'd watch the sun set from the window, play with the toys I'd brought along for him, and read in bed until we fell asleep.

I intended for us to explore other parts of New England, but once school started, I was too busy to plan another weekend getaway. The only trip I took, alone, was to a small town in Vermont, where my friend Jim was completing an artist's residency that culminated in a solo exhibit. He made gowns that resembled priests' cassocks and embroidered the front panels and sleeves with words advocating women's rights. The bed-and-breakfast where I stayed was run by two Episcopalian priests who were married to each other. Their little Siamese cat wandered from room to room, rubbing her head on suitcases, meowing loudly, and demanding to be petted. Tosca, she was called: a tiny diva. I wished I could have brought Oscar but figured he and I would have plenty of time to travel.

Then in February, I came home from teaching and found him drooling, wheezing, and struggling for breath on the floor of my new writing room. The echocardiogram taken at the emergency animal hospital revealed an extra shelf of muscle growing between the chambers of his heart, blocking the blood flow and causing his lungs to fill with fluid. Oscar had a congenital heart defect even though he'd shown no sign of it till now. The veterinary cardiologist said no surgery was available to remove the obstruction, but Oscar might live "for a while" if he could tolerate the medication to keep his lungs clear. First, he had to gain back the weight he'd lost in the three days he'd spent at the hospital inside an oxygen chamber.

Trying to feed Oscar reminded me of my last visit to my grandmother. The morning after our family reunion dinner, I woke up at six and heard her shuffling around in the kitchen. As I snuck out the door in my running clothes, I could smell the toast she was making for me—I was the only one who ate bread instead of rice for breakfast—and I was furious at her for not remembering that I hated eating anything until I'd been up for a few hours. So I went for a long run and returned with just enough time to have a cup of tea before the bus arrived to take me back to the city. My grandmother only wished for my health and long life—the two things she valued most, for which eating was an absolute necessity—but until Oscar became too sick to eat, I didn't understand how heartbreaking it was to have someone you love refuse the food you prepared for them.

Oscar's medication made him dehydrated, so he was placed on a prescription low-sodium diet. He sniffed at the dry food I poured into his bowl and walked away. He could be coaxed into eating the canned version only if I rolled a tiny amount into a ball between my thumb and finger and put it in his mouth like a pill. I'd wait for him to chew and swallow, and then I would stick another food pill into his mouth. What he consumed at each sitting amounted to less than a teaspoon, so we repeated our feeding sessions every few hours. He'd sit in my lap and regard me with great tolerance when I pried open his mouth. He slept a lot, but during the few hours he was awake, he'd follow me around and even bat at the feather toy I dangled in front of him. The end wasn't far off, but I was sure we could still have some good times if only I could find the right food to offer him.

I telephoned the animal hospital's veterinary nutritionist, who suggested preparing my own low-sodium food. A home-cooked meal, she said, would be more palatable to Oscar. She emailed me a recipe that required cooked chicken, but it gave no instructions about how to cook it. I was a vegetarian. I had no experience with cooking chickens. The only person I had ever seen prepare chicken successfully was Henri. Every time we ate together, he'd bake a boneless, skinless chicken breast in a glass pie dish with a squirt of lemon for himself and prepare eggs and grits for me. So I phoned him in Germany, where he was working on a book of poems, and he gave me directions for a lemon-less version. But the pristine chicken breast was more like a sonnet than a piece of meat, and Oscar showed no interest in it whatsoever.

Cat and Bird

Other friends I called offered advice but it was more about sanitation. To prevent salmonella poisoning, they said, I should make sure to clean the knife after cutting raw chicken and refrain from using the same cutting board for fruits and vegetables until I'd washed it in boiling water. They made chicken sound so dangerous that I wondered why more people didn't drop dead from eating it. I finally telephoned Peter, who had grown up in rural Wisconsin, where people were less health-conscious. He said that his mother had used a "roasting bag" to keep the chicken moist.

"Cats don't like healthy low-fat food," he pointed out. "I bet Oscar would love the skin and the fat."

No one else I consulted had ever heard of roasting bags, but I found several packages of them in the paper products aisle of a nearby supermarket. The chicken breast I baked in the bag was dripping with grease. Oscar came to the kitchen while I was trying to cut it. He gobbled up the thumb-sized piece that I put in his bowl. He loved the Wisconsin-style baked chicken breast so much that he ate it even after I mixed it with rice and vitamins and ground it up. For years, I had made detours in grocery stores to avoid seeing the rotisserie chickens rotating behind glass; I had a hard time accepting that each headless lump used to be an actual bird. But now that Oscar was eating without being coaxed, I would have caught, killed, and plucked a chicken with my bare hands.

Oscar's medication worked for two months before he started throwing up and losing weight. At four o'clock on Easter morning, almost at the end of my first year in Cambridge, Oscar left the bed where he was sleeping in my arms. He didn't go very far. He sat slumped against the wall and watched me from five feet away, just like he had done on his first night in Green Bay before he decided to become my cat. I could see his chest heaving with his effort to breathe. He was ready to be no one's cat again. I took him to the emergency hospital, where the veterinarian on call reviewed his file and told me that I was doing the right thing.

It was only three years after Dorian's death, and here I was again, trying to hold on to a dying pet while the vet shaved his paw to find a vein for an injection that would take him away from me.

"Hey, Oscar," I said when the needle went in. "I'm so sorry. I love you."

Afterward, the veterinarian explained the available services for the remains. He said I could choose individual cremation, which would allow me to return and claim the ashes, or group cremation, which would authorize the hospital to dispose of them. Unlike in Green Bay, taking the body home was not an option, and even if it had been, I didn't have friends with backyards where I could bury him. In fact, with Henri in Germany, I didn't know anyone in Boston well enough to even say we were friends.

"I think cremation is gruesome," I told the veterinarian. "I don't want the remains. I want to remember Oscar when he was healthy." I sounded just like Chuck when Dorian was dying. I signed the form authorizing the group cremation, touched Oscar's body one more time, and turned to go. I didn't believe I was making a stoic gesture of acceptance. Leaving his body to strangers had nothing to do with wanting to remember him as a healthy cat. I simply could not imagine living with his ashes in that tiny apartment, in a city where I had no friends.

Cat and Bird

Four years later, I was still living in Cambridge with one more year left at Harvard. Taking a leave of absence with a fellowship halfway through the contract had given me the extra time, but I had no prospects for a job afterward. I needed a ritual to face my fears, and in early June, I drove to the small town of Salem, New Hampshire, to get a tattoo. The tattoo studio was inside a shabby house on a street with a few other studios like it, a couple of tanning salons, and from what I could tell, a couple of biker bars. It was recommended by a very stylish woman in her fifties who worked at a boutique near Harvard Square, but the street reminded me of West Broadway, the biker hangout in Green Bay.

The sign out front featured a huge rainbow-colored parrot, and standing in front of it, I imagined driving back to the apartment where Oscar had climbed onto my futon our first morning together and guided me into the future. He was with me for three years and 1,100 miles before leaving me to finish the journey on my own; he'd been gone a year longer than he was alive. I didn't blame myself for his death, but I regretted how I had allowed him to be cremated without ceremony after he had spent all of his allotted time on earth helping me free myself from the life I had outgrown. I fled from his body because I was overcome by self-pity when I should have been feeling gratitude.

I entered the dilapidated house. The walls were covered with photographs of vines and swords, guns and flowers, Jesus and comic book superheroes cavorting on various people's shoulders, arms, backs, and breasts, and Chinese pictographs signifying everything from happiness to death etched on ankles and wrists. On the coffee table, among the piles of tattoo magazines and comic books, were two birdwatching classics you can find on any birder's bookshelf: *National Geographic Complete Birds of North America* and *Peterson's Field Guide to Eastern Birds.* I didn't understand why these books were in a tattooist's waiting room until I picked up the black binder of ink drawings and discovered birds flying across several pages: hummingbirds, eagles, swallows, seagulls, and cranes navigating their way around pictographs, crosses, vines, and swords.

I clutched an envelope that contained a photograph of Oscar sitting on my suitcase, looking straight into the camera. Oscar spent what turned out to be his only fall and winter in our Cambridge apartment perched in the window, watching the sparrows roosting in the maple trees across the street. The condo association didn't allow us to install bird feeders—for fear of attracting rats, they said—but no one noticed if I placed a handful of sunflower seeds directly on the window ledge. In early winter, a few weeks before Oscar got sick, a dozen tufted titmice flew back and forth between the bare maple branches and the window, picking off one sunflower seed at a time and returning to the trees to crack it open against the bark. I had never before seen these tiny, mouse-colored birds with large black eyes and crests on their heads, but I recognized them from my *Peterson's Field Guide.* Small, active, and gregarious, they made loud buzzing calls like a chorus of Siamese cats. Oscar's head moved back and forth with their movement from the trees to the window, the window to the trees. Unlike the sparrows and nuthatches we saw every day, titmice swarmed our window all that afternoon and then vanished, but they briefly returned to my window every winter.

"You can add them to your life list," I told Oscar.

My grief for Oscar was different than it was for Dorian. Dorian didn't need a commemorative object or gesture because

Cat and Bird

he had nearly two decades to influence the course of my life and leave an indelible impression on everyone who knew me. But Oscar had the life span of a migratory bird: he guided me across the country and then he was gone, leaving our story unfinished. This tattoo was a way of completing the circle, like embroidering a family crest on a formal kimono. The tattooist inked it on the back of my neck: Oscar sitting with his long tail wrapped around his front paws, his blue eyes intensely alert. Tattoos are ritualized scars, and the image on my back is a pun on Oscar's name: O-scar. Its circular shape commemorates the way he walked around every room in which we had spent the night and made it into a home. If I could travel back in time, knowing how the future would turn out, I would point to him again, where he sat beside his sleeping brothers with his eyes wide open, and say, "That one." Now and for the rest of my life, I had Oscar to watch my back so I could keep moving forward.

Chapter Nine

Ernest and Algernon

After Oscar's death, I climbed the four flights of stairs to my apartment in silence, only to step through the door into deeper silence. Soon, the school year was over, and at every gathering I attended, I listened to plans being made by other guests for their summer sojourns to Paris or Florence. My new colleagues were shocked to hear that the only foreign country I'd ever been to was my home country of Japan, though I didn't reveal that I had been there just three times in twenty-three years and that the last time I was there, I made sure I would never have to see my family again.

I only got in touch with Hiroshi, Michiko, and Jumpei during my first trip to Japan because my other relatives would feel awkward if I didn't. We had dinner at a Chinese restaurant, where Hiroshi smoked nonstop, Michiko badmouthed the few people we all knew, and Jumpei sat silently drinking chilled sake. On my second trip, when I went to meet my Japanese publisher, my brother was out of town, so Hiroshi, Michiko, and I met again for dinner, though at a different restaurant. After that, I stopped answering the letters Hiroshi sent me periodically to criticize my modest teaching job and childless marriage. I had no idea he was ill until Jumpei called me one February morning in 1994 to say he had died. He urged me to book a flight to Kobe. There was no way I could get to Japan in time for the funeral scheduled the next day; what I had told my father on the morning of my departure was coming true. Still, Jumpei insisted our family would be truly disgraced if I didn't show up, even late, to burn incense at the altar in Michiko's apartment.

Cat and Bird

As it turned out, the real purpose of this third visit was for me to sign the numerous legal documents required to designate Michiko as the sole heir to my father's estate. In Japan, few people leave wills. By law, 50 percent of a dead man's estate goes to his spouse; the other 50 percent is divided equally among the children. But most families choose just one person—usually the oldest son—to keep their wealth and status intact. Jumpei had never lived in his own apartment or held a regular job. He operated an import-export business of South American folk art—a venture kept afloat by our family's money. He spent most of his time traveling abroad, and for the few months he was in Japan, he stayed with Hiroshi and Michiko. My father had left enough money for all of us to live comfortably. If I signed the forms (ominously known as "renunciation documents"), Michiko could claim all of Hiroshi's assets but continue to support Jumpei, who eventually would inherit whatever was left.

I arrived two days after the funeral, checked into a hotel, and took a cab to the condominium where Hiroshi and Michiko had been living for several years. Michiko showed me into the spare bedroom where she had set up an altar with my father's picture next to a painting of Buddhist heaven. I lit an incense stick, rang the bell that supposedly summoned the spirits, closed my eyes, and bowed my head as expected. Michiko and I sat side by side in silence. After what seemed like a respectful duration, I opened my eyes. Michiko bowed deeper before straightening her back. Then she reached under the floor cushion she was sitting on, pulled out a thick envelope, handed it to me, and motioned for me to leave. She closed the door, presumably to commune alone with my father's spirit, and my brother, who had been waiting in the living room, explained that for each asset my father left—from the apartment to the smallest checking account used for daily expenses—I had to sign a document to say that it could go to Michiko. Of course he had already signed his.

"Banks have such stupid requirements," he said. "Until you sign your papers, *Okasan* (meaning "Mother," that's what he always called Michiko) can't even take money out of her checking account because it's officially in Father's name. I lent her some cash." He laughed at the absurdity of him—the child—giving money to his "mother."

Maybe Michiko was expecting me to sign the papers then and there and present them to her in front of my father's altar, but I went back to the hotel, leaving my brother to tell her I needed time to consider. But I'd already made up my mind. I sat on the bed, opened the envelope, took out the forms, and signed them all. I didn't comply to help my brother or to spare our family the embarrassment of a lawsuit to enforce the inheritance law. As long as Hiroshi was alive, my freedom had felt provisional. Years after I had become a US citizen, I had nightmares about being dragged back to Japan to live with him and Michiko, and now, I didn't want to be tied to Hiroshi through his money. Once I handed over the documents, I was in effect disowning my family. First, I had abandoned the country of my birth; now, I was abandoning my birthright.

In the five years since that visit, I hadn't heard from Michiko or Jumpei, and they no longer knew where I lived. I had no desire to travel to Japan, but every night when I returned to my apartment, I was stunned by the silence in Oscar's absence. If I could spend the summer alone in a foreign country, I figured, I wouldn't be afraid to come home to an empty apartment.

I didn't want to go to a city where I couldn't speak the

language, so I settled on London and Dublin. I bought a stack of guidebooks and read them every evening while eating the simplest meals I could throw together—dry toast and shredded lettuce. With Dorian and then with Oscar, I would cook a meal and set a place for myself on the floor with a placemat, a cloth napkin, and silverware so the cat could sit next to me without jumping up on the table. I didn't offer table scraps indiscriminately, but each cat had a few favorites he was allowed to sample: butter, tortilla chips, and roasted peanuts for Dorian, yogurt and bananas for Oscar. Dinner with them had been an occasion, a chance to put aside the day's activities and enjoy the food, the quiet. But now I understood why people ate Chinese takeout from cardboard boxes while standing over the kitchen sink. Sitting alone with a plate of food in front of me, I felt self-conscious in my own company.

Trying to write in an empty apartment was even more daunting. I had turned the small bedroom into a study, with the desk by the window and the couch nearby, where Oscar could sit to watch over my writing. At night, he and I had slept on the futon in the living room because writing, more than sleeping, required its own special room that no one else ever entered. But with Oscar gone, I sat at my desk only to stare out the window, unable to write a word, even in my journal.

In my last years with Dorian, I finished the young adult novel inspired by the birds in Kobe and the memoir about my trip to Japan. Afterward, I knew I had said my last goodbye to Japan in my writing. With Oscar beside me in Green Bay, I started a novel set in rural Wisconsin, featuring a weaver who had grown up in Osaka. The story had a cat in it who was tiny and energetic like Oscar and singularly devoted to my main character the way Dorian had been to me.

I tried to picture myself sitting alone in a hotel room in London or Dublin and picking up the manuscript I hadn't touched since Oscar got sick. Henri was back from Germany and applying for travel fellowships and summer residencies. Although he lived alone, he never wrote in his Boston apartment. All the poems in his last book were composed away from home. He said that travel helped him clear his head; leaving one place for another inspired him to explore new ideas. I could use a fresh perspective too, but I already had a change of scenery from my cross-country move. Flying to London and sitting in a hotel room wasn't going to help me start over.

For me, traveling only intensified the feeling of transience. My whole life after my mother's death had been spent in places where I didn't belong, beginning with my father's house. No matter where I went, I faced a barrage of contradictory impressions and memories. My mother's depression had started with a move she regretted. In our hilltop neighborhood, the houses were set far apart, and most of the women who lived in them with their retired husbands were older than my mother. Unable to summon the energy to make new friends or pursue any hobbies by herself, my mother filled her journal with the same thoughts over and over again: we should have never left our old house; she was a failure as a wife and mother, a burden to everyone.

Now I was also holed up in a new place that didn't feel like home, in a city where I didn't know anyone. My neighborhood in Cambridge, with its brick buildings and narrow sidewalks, was dark even during the day. My mother had complained about trees that cast shadows into her kitchen all day long. I felt hemmed in too. But I didn't have it in me to relive the decisions that had brought me there, to blame myself and conclude that my whole life was worthless. I knew it wasn't the move to Massachusetts that was making me sad. I was grieving for Oscar and for Dorian and for my mother and grandmother and everyone I had ever loved and lost and all the homes I had left behind. Still, underneath the sadness, I had an almost ruthless determination to keep going. That was the difference between my mother and me, the daughter who placed her mother's bones in a jar and walked away. Surviving required stepping into the future and abandoning everything and everyone that had come before. If that was a form of betrayal, I had to accept it all the same.

Since Oscar's death, I hadn't felt motivated to decorate my apartment, explore the city, or get to know the colleagues and neighbors I'd met. My writing room was the only place on the planet where I could make sense of my confusing thoughts and transform them into words worth keeping. But I couldn't turn chaos into order without a guardian to protect and fortify my solitude. I decided against traveling to the United Kingdom and to stay and begin my search for another guardian, or two.

With Dorian and then with Oscar, I'd had an all-absorbing, one-on-one relationship, more like a marriage than any of the half-hearted attempts I'd made with humans. Dorian had protected me, and Oscar had guided me into the second half of my adult life, but alone in a new place without him, I didn't know how to start the future I'd envisioned. A thousand miles away from my last adopted home, I was floating like Momo Taro across the sea. To continue my journey, I too needed a team of helpers.

I remembered Tosca, the Siamese cat at the Vermont bed-and-breakfast, so I called the Episcopalian priests to find out where she had come from. Her breeder, who lived in another part of Vermont, told me she expected to have kittens available in a few months and promised to reserve a male for me. That's when I knew for certain that I needed two cats but that the other cat should come from the Midwest. Together, they would unite the two halves of my adult life like two pillars of support. I was referred to a breeder just outside of Minneapolis, where I'd spent the summer with Oscar.

"I have a kitten who's ready to go right now," the breeder said when I called her. "He's a very handsome boy, sixteen weeks old."

I decided to name the two cats Ernest and Algernon, after the best friends in Oscar Wilde's *The Importance of Being Earnest.* In the play, the two men grow up in separate homes but turn out to be brothers. After Algernon and Ernest joined me, I learned that they were distantly related—their breeding charts had one cat in common going back five generations. And now, through me, they were together as brothers, just as Wilde would have intended.

Unlike dogs, cats don't need their owner to be the leader of the pack on a daily basis. Dorian and Oscar had both refused to "obey" me, as when Dorian terrorized my friends and Oscar transformed our cross-country drive into the noisiest, most harrowing hours I'd ever spent behind the wheel. Even so, all along, I was the one who plotted the course of our lives: we moved when I got married, divorced, and changed jobs, and I decided what was best for their health and safety. Like the characters I put in my stories, my cats often surprised me by having their own minds, but ultimately, I was in control. The most rewarding part of our interactions was the give-and-take that became necessary when their personalities asserted themselves, challenging me to make new discoveries and accommodations. My role was to create an environment in which they were nurtured and protected so they could develop into the complex characters they were meant to be.

Cat and Bird

Ernest, a blue-point Siamese, arrived on a midnight flight from Minneapolis. He was inside a huge plastic carrier that was hand-carried off the plane and brought to the baggage area where I was waiting. The sticker on the side of the carrier spelled out "LIVE ANIMAL" in red letters. He hissed at me and spent the next three days hiding, then emerged from under the couch to jump into my lap, where he slept all afternoon—exhausted, apparently, from the effort it took to be so recalcitrant. He would grow up to be just like the older brother in Wilde's play: picky and dignified, a stickler for decorum, every bit the country gentleman. Guests would admire his blue-gray marking and pale blue eyes while he sat on his high perch and regarded them with great skepticism.

Algernon, a seal point with a black mask, vest, boots, and mitts, was—like his namesake—a freewheeling man about town, carefree and insouciant. On the day I picked him up from his breeder in Vermont, he slept through the entire four-hour drive and woke up purring as I was trying to parallel park. Because both Ernest and Algernon grew up with other cats and came to me only three months apart, they got along from the start and soon became more like Siamese twins than Siamese cats. The only time they weren't conjoined was when they were attached to me, one in my arms and the other on my lap. One light and one dark, like salt and pepper, they were a matched set. They kept me doubly homebound, exactly as I wished.

Algernon teetered on his hind legs like a dancing monkey when he reached with his paw to bat at the feathers I dangled over his head. He played hard, got tired, and sat down while Ernest, who'd been lurking behind the furniture, would step out to dominate the game. Algernon was a pure athlete, Ernest a strategist. He could play a slow, careful game of chase-the-feather for nearly an hour. One evening, a research fellow from Korea, who was subleasing my neighbor's apartment, was right behind me as we came up the steps. When I opened my door, she saw Ernest waiting for me in the foyer and blurted out, "Oh! Is that a dog or a cat?" Maybe she was responding to the way he was sitting by the door and looking straight at me, or else his coloring put her in mind of a little white dog. Either way, her question encapsulated how lucky I was to be spending the summer with Ernest and Algernon instead of traveling alone overseas. Like Momo Taro, I had found the companions I needed to continue my story: two cats at my side who even resembled the monkey and the dog, and flocks of birds that came to my window and could stand for the flush of a pheasant in the sky overhead.

Most folk stories are about the hero's departure from home and his adventures abroad. In the story of Momo Taro, we glimpse the humble peasant's cottage he grew up in as he walks away, but we never find out how long he lived there with the old couple before he embarked on his adventure (although I did always wonder: how many years did it take a boy born from a peach to become a normal-sized person?). At the end, his triumphant homecoming only gets a few sentences; his adoptive parents welcome him, and the villagers praise him for recovering the stolen treasure. No one knows what happened next, though I always assumed that Momo Taro and his helpers eventually set out on another adventure.

For Momo Taro, home was a base camp where he could gather his strength and prepare for his journey. For my mother, home was a prison where she contemplated her failures and decided to die. My story so far had been a sequel to hers: a saga of escape. What I had accomplished along the way—leaving Japan, getting an education, becoming a writer—felt more like defensive tactics than successes worth celebrating. But now, two years older than my mother was when she died, I was safe from the misery that killed her.

With Ernest and Algernon in my life, I would never feel trapped and isolated in my own house. Even while living in Japan, or in a small town in Wisconsin where people also believed that a woman without a husband and children was nothing, I hadn't questioned my choice to be different, and that was because my mother had prepared me. The best way to honor her was to make a home as a single, childless woman in a new city. It wasn't enough to be content alone in my apartment, as I had been back in Wisconsin. This time, I had to put down roots in the community, even if they were temporary. Oscar showed me how to treat every new place as a home, and Momo Taro taught me how to use food to transform strangers into friends.

I wasn't nervous about cooking for company, but it seemed awkward to invite people I scarcely knew to my tiny apartment. I relied on Ernest and Algernon to help me break the ice.

"I live with two amazing cats," I told people. "You should come over to dinner and meet them. They're great cooks. They can even bake bread."

Unlike in the Midwest, where friends stopped by unannounced and stayed to eat whatever you were cooking, dinner invitations in Cambridge were major overtures. People often said they'd love to come but they were too busy, or they canceled at the last minute. Without the cats, I wouldn't have had the resilience to keep trying.

"We'll be in touch again," I always said, meaning the cats and I would offer another chance. I finally understood why many married people said "we" and "us" automatically while discussing everything from their social plans to life goals. The plural pronoun was very effective in glossing over anxiety, wounded pride, or self-consciousness.

In Green Bay, if you met one person who liked you, then that person would introduce you to a dozen friends who got together regularly. Whatever the activity, it was casual and easy to plan. My friends and I would go to a movie every Tuesday night. We'd sit in the middle of an otherwise empty theater and take up the whole row, like birds lined up on a branch. After the movie, we'd move around town in a compact flock the way cedar waxwings do from orchard to orchard, devouring the fruit. If someone decided not to show up or left early, there was no reason to take it personally.

I could never have organized a movie night in Cambridge if my life depended on it. No two people were free on the same night, and even if they were, every single person had a strong opinion about which movie to see and where to sit once we got there. People only socialized in groups on special occasions around a significant event; they didn't get together just to pass the time. Making friends on the East Coast was like trying to tame a feral cat by putting out food in the farthest corner of the yard and then moving the bowl closer to the porch, inch by inch, until you had convinced the animal to come into the house.

Ernest and Algernon kept me company while I cooked. When guests arrived, Algernon sat in their lap while Ernest stretched out on the highest perch, dangling one elegant paw over the couch. Eventually, Algernon would leave the guest's lap and come to mine. Then Ernest would jump off the perch, push Algernon out of the way, and make a huge production of settling himself in my lap. Algernon resigned himself to curling up next to me. The cats must have looked like twin moons orbiting around me. In truth, Ernest was the sun, I was the earth, and Algernon was the moon. Either way, we were our own galaxy. One of my colleagues was so impressed with Algernon that she put him in her novel, a cameo appearance as a little Siamese cat who walked from room to room, observing and keeping everyone's secrets.

The friends I made in Cambridge were writers or artists who held temporary teaching jobs like mine. They had a habit of stopping me in the middle of a conversation to ask, "How do you feel about that?"—a question no one asked in the Midwest, where it was assumed that on the rare occasion people wanted to discuss their feelings, they would bring up the topic on their own. In Cambridge, if I said, "I have no idea how I feel. I'll have to think about it for a while," only a few of my new friends laughed. Most were annoyed by my unwillingness to confide in them about problems I preferred to solve on my own. Maintaining friendships required a frequent negotiation of the boundaries between privacy and honesty. It was exhausting, but with those who didn't give up on me, or I on them, we eventually developed a closer, more lasting friendship than I'd had with anyone in Green Bay, except Jim.

But I knew that staying in Cambridge would never be permanent. Although numerous universities and colleges were within driving distance, tenured teaching positions were scarce. Many of my predecessors at Harvard had remained in the area at the end of their contract by obtaining fellowships and lectureships from different institutions every few years. But I didn't love Cambridge enough to continue living there on such precarious terms. Just like in Kobe, people only socialized with others with similar professional status. I blended into the crowd near Harvard Square, not because there were other Asian people there but because I too spoke, dressed, and carried myself like someone with multiple years of postsecondary education. We were all disconcertingly the same, and the sameness led to the scrutiny of the smallest differences. My friends worried about not accomplishing as much as others in their circle in every area of life: career, social life, travel, entertainment, fitness, even trivial things like how much or how little they slept. My mother had berated herself for not being able to take charge of our new home and her neglectful husband. When she said she was a failure, she was comparing herself with countless other women, and she felt ashamed for not being as resilient or resourceful. Although I never had that anxiety, it was exhausting to live in an atmosphere of constant judgment and self-scrutiny.

At work parties, where colleagues compared their stories about far-flung places, I became nostalgic for the seedy bar in Green Bay where my friends passed around jars of pickled hot peppers that someone's brother had sent from Kansas City, debating whether Irish beer should be chilled or consumed at room temperature. Sitting in the annual condo association meeting with neighbors who were lawyers and architects, I thought of a former neighbor, the part-time English teacher who played the cello in the civic symphony and slept on a camping mattress among bins of found recyclables. I had no desire to live in a small town again, but I wanted to settle in a city where people could pursue their chosen lifestyle, however eccentric, without pressure or judgment—the one ideal I preserved from my marriage to Chuck.

After three years at Harvard, I was offered a one-year fellowship back in Milwaukee that would allow me to write full time, so

Cat and Bird

I took a leave of absence and moved west again to live a mile from my old neighborhood. I had finished the novel about the Japanese weaver; now I wanted to write about weaving itself, a craft I had learned while living in Green Bay. I didn't know any weavers in Cambridge, but in Milwaukee, I could take weaving classes at a local craft center. I could meet up with Jim in Chicago to look at tapestries in museums. I could also reconnect with friends from graduate school and meet new people through bird hikes at the nature center and through a knitting circle that got together every week. Although I was only two hours away from Green Bay, Milwaukee was a diverse city, so no one stared at me or asked me about Japan; it was the closest thing I had to a hometown.

Every morning, I ran along the lakeshore back to my old neighborhood and passed the building where Dorian first came to live with me. The brownstone—built in the early twentieth century just like my place in Cambridge—had been turned into a condominium, and occasionally, there was a realty company's sign on the front lawn. I pictured myself living in a three-bedroom apartment with Ernest and Algernon, owning the whole place this time.

Lake Michigan was a constant presence in the city; even when I couldn't see it, I felt its proximity in the light overhead and the air around me. Running along the bluff with the water spread below me, I felt like a bird charting its navigation route. I had spent most of my adulthood within a few miles of the lake; now, after a three-year absence, it had once again become my point of reference. I didn't want to leave it behind again, so I contacted several colleges and universities in Milwaukee and Chicago, hoping that one of them might offer me a job. But in 2002—a year into the dot-com recession—the best any school could promise was to consider me when the economy recovered.

I would have been more disappointed if Ernest hadn't been so miserable the whole year. He hated the apartment in Milwaukee, which occupied the entire ground floor of a two-story house. He was accustomed to a 440-square-foot studio with all five windows facing east and offering the same views of maple trees and rooftops from every room, of passing cars and people walking four stories below. Now he was stuck on the street level, in a space three times the size and surrounded by windows on all sides. He couldn't stop running from room to room, alarmed and gripped by everything he saw: neighbors and their dogs, our landlady in the yard, kids going to and returning from school.

Algernon would spend his afternoons lounging on the cat tree I had moved from Cambridge and placed next to my writing desk. Ernest would check on us as he patrolled the apartment, stopping to rub against my legs, jumping on the perch to wrestle Algernon awake, then leaping down to resume his rounds. When he was finally exhausted, he'd settle next to Algernon and fall asleep. Their bodies, interlocked, looked like a yin and yang sign.

Then, in April, Ernest began spending most of his time in the bedroom. I was hoping that after ten months he might be settling down, but he was actually just watching a pair of robins above the window building their nest, laying their eggs, and hatching little baby birds. Algernon didn't even notice them, but for two weeks, Ernest was glued to the sight of the adult birds flying back and forth to feed their young, their wings casting flickering shadows on the wall. They were so tenacious and territorial; the male sang from dawn to dusk to declare his dominion. I don't know if Ernest understood that the two baby robins, whose heads would poke out periodically, were potentially his food or if he was miffed that the parents were invading his viewing space.

Cat and Bird

On the day the fledglings left the nest, I returned from an errand and found the adult birds screeching and dive-bombing my landlady's terrier. I chased the dog around the yard, cornered him by my dining room window, and pried his mouth open, but the fledgling was no longer moving. There was a gash across its mottled chest and one of its legs was broken.

My landlady had been sitting in a lawn chair, covering her ears.

"Those birds build a nest under our second-floor deck every year," she said. "Toby always gets a few."

"I can't believe you came out here with him, knowing that," I responded, not caring how rude I sounded. "Even my cat knew those birds were about to fledge."

My landlady gathered the catalogs she'd been reading and shoved them into the tote bag at her feet.

The adult birds gave up and left. They had no idea I was trying to rescue their offspring. To them I was just another predator, larger and more aggressive than the dog. I hoped they found the other fledgling wherever he was hiding and escorted him to safety. I watched the landlady call her dog and walk with him into the house through the back door, and then I got a shovel from the garage and buried the dead bird in her flower bed. Back in our apartment, Ernest sat crouched in the kitchen. Maybe he'd been following me from window to window while the dog, the birds, and I rampaged through the yard. He was clearly tormented by the confusing events going on outside. I should have been more sympathetic, but I started laughing.

"You should lighten up, Ernest," I said. "Don't be so glum."

Two months later, when we headed back east, Ernest hollered every minute of the drive, refused to eat his food, paraded unhappily around the motel room at night, and even peed in the car. But as soon as we returned to our Cambridge apartment, he leapt out of the pet carrier, purring, while Algernon, who had tried so hard to be a good traveler—dutifully eating his food and using the litter box and sleeping in the motel rooms' strange beds—clung to me, his whole body trembling.

Over the last three days on the phone, my friend Mako, who'd come over to help me unload the car, had been following Ernest's operatic howling complaints across seven states. She'd grown up with cats in New Jersey, Tokyo, and New York; she had even had one when she lived in New Zealand for a year. She was as devoted to her cat, Miranda, as I was to mine, and we had other things in common, like both being Japanese-American writers. She watched Ernest, ecstatic to reclaim his home, circle the foyer with his tail up, then flop down on the floor, stretch himself luxuriously, and roll around with his legs extended. She said she'd never seen a cat look so smug. My sublease tenant had moved out the day before. To a cat's sensitive nose, the premises must have smelled like a stranger's clothes and books, but Ernest didn't care. He was telling me that this was where we belonged. I pretended to be irritated with him, but I was secretly relieved. His happiness counterbalanced my worries about returning to Cambridge, where I only had two years left on my nonrenewable contract.

In October of the following year, I stood in line at the post office with over forty envelopes stuffed with job applications. Because every school asked for different materials, each envelope had to be weighed separately. The sole clerk working the counter sent me to the back of the line after every five envelopes so he could serve other customers who kept arriving.

Cat and Bird

Each batch of envelopes was like a small flock of birds flying across the country. "Don't get shot down," I used to call to the geese passing over the tennis courts where Chuck and I played in Wisconsin. "Survive and prosper!"

The job prospects that had looked dire the year I spent in Milwaukee looked even worse now. When I left a tenured job for the temporary position at Harvard, I didn't foresee that the economy would hit a slump shortly afterward and many universities would institute hiring freezes. Just like after graduate school, I had to apply for any job that would give me financial security and allow me time to write.

Nearly every night after I sent out the applications, I had the same four dreams that had been on a loop inside my head over many years: I opened my mouth to speak and all my teeth fell out; I chopped off my hair and didn't recognize my face in the mirror; I was trapped inside a strange house, only to find a secret door that led back to my father's house; and, worst of all, my cats and I moved to a new apartment where someone had left the door open, and the cats had wandered away and were lost or possibly dead. I woke up clutching Algernon, who would be sleeping under the covers in my arms. Ernest would be pacing around the room because I had accidentally kicked him off the bed.

"Don't worry, just a dream," I said. It was obvious—probably even to them—that I was trying to reassure myself.

So I was relieved to get early campus interviews in South Carolina and Northern Virginia and to be offered both jobs right away. In Columbia, South Carolina, the Confederate flag was still displayed on the grounds of the statehouse, but the job in Northern Virginia made it possible to live in Washington, DC, a city I had visited a dozen times over the years. The university would hire me with tenure so I would never have to move again.

I accepted, withdrew the dozens of pending applications, and started planning my move.

When it came time to hold an open house for my condo, I took the cats to spend the weekend with Brighde, a playwright I'd taught with the previous year. A single woman my age, she now lived in Providence, Rhode Island. On the drive over, Ernest meowed in the raspy voice he only used when he was truly upset. Frazzled by his distress, I reneged on my promise to take her out to dinner and suggested we stay in, order pizza, and watch a movie instead. Brighde humored me; at the time, she didn't have a pet of her own and had no way of understanding my preoccupation with the safety and comfort of my cats. Ernest paced around her living room nonstop, huffing and grunting, while Algernon slept in my lap. The minute we were home again, Ernest rolled around on the floor just like he did after our Milwaukee sojourn, having no idea that the open house had resulted in an offer I could accept. I then booked a flight to DC, promising him I would find us a permanent place to live so we'd only have to move once.

When people talked about companionship as the mainstay of marriage, they meant a married couple could experience change together but remain held in place by their relationship to each other—like tandem skydivers falling through the atmosphere. That's how I looked at my move. Finding an apartment in Washington would have terrified me if I didn't have Ernest and Algernon. What makes a real estate decision overwhelming is the infinity of choices. Fortunately, my cats narrowed my options from the start. I could only live in a building that allowed pets, and there was no way Ernest could be on the ground floor again. These restrictions transformed the search into a challenge I could tackle: a puzzle instead of a conundrum, not unlike every story or essay I shaped into being. Each act of creation, whether for a home or a piece of writing, begins with establishing the strictures and separating what is possible from what can never be.

The last apartment the real estate agent showed me was in a brownstone of similar size and age as my Cambridge condo. It too was situated on the top floor facing east. It even had the same kind of windows, with wavy glass and a pulley system. The moment I walked in, I knew exactly where to put my desk: next to the window in the alcove adjacent to the kitchen, a spot originally intended as a dining nook. I could picture Ernest sitting there and looking down at the trees—crepe myrtle, cedar, and magnolia. There were no sugar maples, but after all, he wasn't an arborist. The layout of the whole apartment was nearly identical to our current home, so I could arrange most of the furniture in the same configuration, using the living room as both a sitting and dining area.

Ernest meowed for the entire drive and huffed around the New Jersey motel room where we stayed the night. But once we arrived in the new apartment, he curled up on the blanket I'd brought from our old place and fell asleep. After the furniture was delivered and every piece was arranged in its rightful spot, Ernest rewarded my efforts by settling right in. He had given me an excuse to recreate our Cambridge apartment, and though it may have seemed as if I was placating him, I too needed to neutralize the move by ensuring that my territory and daily routine remained unchanged, that my life and my cats were protected and contained within the one place I knew.

My street was lined with ornamental cherry trees, their small dark berries hidden behind leaves. Almost every residence, including my new building, had a hedge of Japanese laurel, with their waxy green leaves spotted yellow, a red maple, or a magnolia in the front yard and groves of bamboo out back. Garden flowers that barely tolerated the climates of Green Bay and Boston thrived here: azaleas that looked electrified in the sun, blue and pink hydrangeas as well as the hardier white variety. Block after block, I found myself running past the trees and bushes of my childhood.

The co-op had no ban against growing flowers and feeding birds on the window ledge, so I bought window boxes and planted petunias, salvias, snapdragons, and other summer annuals my mother used to grow. After a hummingbird buzzed up to the window while I was watering the flowers, I installed a sugar water feeder that provided a perch. House sparrows, ubiquitous the world over, came to the seed feeder, along with a dozen other species of North American songbirds.

The atmosphere at the co-op was more relaxed than at the Cambridge condo. Neighbors knocked on one another's door to borrow eggs for baking or quarters for the laundry. The cats and I got to work getting to know them better by inviting them to dinner, starting naturally with the cat owners on our floor. There were fifteen cats distributed among the twenty-seven units in the building, and their owners were mostly women my age who worked at museums, libraries, or government offices. Soon, we were meeting for coffee and taking care of each other's cats. We had potluck dinners, movie nights, and craft get-togethers, the most memorable of which involved making felt ornaments with hair saved from our cats' weekly brushings.

Few women (or men) I met in Cambridge cooked regularly, much less baked bread or knitted sweaters. In Washington, I had friends and neighbors who were lifelong knitters, with whom I could exchange patterns and visit yarn stores. Finally, after two years of making false starts on a book about weaving, I realized I should be writing about knitting. Weaving is an exacting discipline that isolates each weaver at her loom. Knitting, by contrast, is a hobby easily pursued alone or in a group, by practitioners of various skill levels. Writing a book about knitting—both my own experience and the rich history of the craft—would allow me to explore what it meant to make a home as a single woman and belong to a community of women past and present who had made diverse and unique choices of their own.

The dining nook I'd converted into my studio adjoined a galley kitchen where generations of women had cooked. Our brownstone had been a rental building from 1923, when its initial construction was finalized, to 1985, when it became a co-op. Most of the recent residents were single women and childless couples, but all the apartments had once been occupied by young married couples with children, or widowed women who lived with their relatives. In the 1940 census, every adult female in the building was identified as a homemaker, including the few women who had outside jobs. The husbands (the "heads" of the family) worked as architects, lawyers, automobile salesmen, bank tellers, or clerks. Life during the Second World War couldn't have been easy for these families, especially after May 1942, when supply shortages forced the US government to institute food rations. The women from our building would have had to use stamps to obtain restricted items such as sugar, coffee, meat, cheese, fats, and canned milk.

I remembered my grandmother's stories about her struggles to feed her family during the war. She had to sell her heirloom kimonos in order to buy food on the black market once the rationed items ran out. "Everything I had turned into rice," was how she put it. Although they were on opposite sides of the war, my grandmother and the women in our building—my residential ancestors—had shared the same worries about feeding their families.

I had never gone hungry with no food in my house, but one of my favorite writers, M. F. K. Fisher, gave me a glimpse inside the life of a 1940s homemaker. In her 1942 book, *How to Cook a Wolf*, she remarks, "There are very few men and women, I suspect, who cooked and marketed their way through the past war without losing forever some of the nonchalant extravagance of the twenties." She laments that "eggs and cream and cinnamon, not to mention fuel needed for long slow bakings, have suddenly become rare and precious things to be used cunningly for a whole meal or a weekly treat."

Fisher published *How to Cook a Wolf* at age thirty-four, a year after the suicide of her second husband, the artist Dillwyn Parrish. She was married one more time, but her third marriage, like the first, didn't last very long. Once widowed and twice divorced at forty-two, she spent the next four decades as a single woman. Many of her stories are about eating alone, both in private and in public.

"I taught myself to enjoy being alone," she writes in *The Gastronomical Me*. "If I must be alone, I refuse to be alone as if it were something weak and distasteful, like convalescence."

Although Fisher traveled and socialized widely, shuttling between the US and Europe, she considered a secluded house she owned in the country in California to be her true home. In her later years, she was often photographed with a Siamese cat in her lap, his light gray fur matching her silver hair. She was a contemporary of my grandmother's; both spent their last years alone in the 1980s and early 1990s. I never saw my grandmother cooking, or doing anything else, when she wasn't surrounded by a houseful of relatives visiting her, but I remembered the small dishes of rice, vegetables, and tea she prepared every morning for the spirits of our ancestors and placed on the Buddhist altar along with the offering of incense and flowers from her garden. I wanted to believe that she too found solace and dignity in her quiet house in the country.

In the early evening, when I sat down on the bed to read or watch television, Ernest and Algernon would climb into my lap and curl together on my legs. In many Impressionist paintings, rowers sit with their legs stretched out with a slight bend at the knees. My legs were in a similar position to make room for both cats as the three of us settled into another leisurely evening at home. I pictured us boating on a calm lake, admiring the lily pads as iridescent dragonflies streamed by. I had never before felt so settled or content.

Ernest and Algernon were no longer kittens but still young. Even when they were diagnosed with feline inflammatory disease (IBD)—akin to Crohn's disease in humans—the veterinarian assured me it was a common chronic condition that could be managed long-term with diet and medication. After the years I spent working with birds—a few of whom refused to open their mouths when I approached them and had to be force-fed— getting a cat to swallow a pill presented no challenge.

To force-feed a reluctant bird, you had to insert the tip of your thumb and forefinger into the rubbery corners of their mouths and press with just the right amount of force to pop open their mouths without breaking their beak; then you had to insert the syringe and shoot the food past their trachea, careful not to suffocate them. With Ernest and Algernon, prying open their mouths took no special skill. Unlike a bird's beak, a cat's mouth is huge and strong; it has sharp teeth and a sandpaper tongue. I found it almost comical to stick in my thumb and forefinger, drop the pill, close their mouths, and stroke their throats to make them swallow. The whole procedure took only a minute for each cat. Ernest, who was the picture of dignity and elegance, bolted when he sensed I was about to give him the pill, but he only ran around for a minute before allowing himself to be caught and went limp in my arms and assumed a resigned expression.

Algernon, who looked even more like a monkey as he got older and his markings became more distinct, would sit at my feet and watch while I pilled Ernest. He was either more accepting of his fate, or he believed that only Ernest was getting the pill; either way, he never led me on a chase. When I laid him belly up in my lap and picked up his medicine, he'd raise one chocolate-colored paw in protest, claws retracted, but he wouldn't push my hand away; the gesture resembled the benign desultory wave of the Japanese *maneki-neko* mascot in a store window. The pill routine became a docility demonstration that my cats and I would perform to entertain guests. To further alleviate their symptoms, I tried various "novel proteins" (duck, rabbit, venison) and then a formula whose proteins had been enzymatically broken down to be less irritating to their stomachs.

By the time their IBD worsened, we had been in Washington for five years, and the cats were ten years old. First Algernon, then Ernest, began throwing up more frequently and losing weight. That's when I started giving them subcutaneous fluids and vitamin D shots. I abhorred needles and had to steel myself for every shot or blood draw, but I had no problem putting the cats in my lap, pinching their skin, and inserting a hydration needle to treat their dehydration. When the tip went in correctly, the slight resistance felt right, like an embroidery needle sliding into thick linen fabric. The water would begin to flow, and the cat would close his eyes and purr. I would sit with them every morning and watch the line of water descending.

Our apartment was a fortress of safety. I had installed central air before we moved in so I wouldn't have to leave the windows open with the old screens that didn't look entirely secure. If someone gave me flowers, I left them in the lobby on top of the decorative cabinet that was too high for any cat to jump on because I had heard that a friend's cat had died from eating lilies, which are toxic to felines. I so frightened the cleaning ladies with my obsession for safety that they once called Gail, my neighbor who had a set of my keys, and asked her to put away the cleaning solutions they had left on the counter by mistake; the women were halfway home when they remembered and couldn't reach me by phone. Gail laughed about my vigilance because I'm only reasonably cautious about my own health. I feared the worst when it came to my cats. No amount of vigilance could protect them from dying before I was ready to let them go.

No matter which room we were in at the animal hospital, Algernon would trot back and forth across the speckled linoleum floor, from the chair by the door to the chair against the desk, bumping and rubbing his head on a chair leg. I'd crouch on the floor, chanting, "Defense, defense," and I would wave my arms. Algernon would keep coming, so I'd crab-walk backward and move out of the way at the last moment. When his head touched the chair leg, I'd call out, "Two points for Algernon!" Then we'd turn around and head for the other chair, with Algernon prancing forward and me retreating. Both baskets were his to score, and if he barreled into me, no fouls were called. Only when he stopped in the middle of the room and reversed his course would I announce, "A big turnover" and reach above his head to tap the chair leg. "Finally, two points for me."

The veterinarian would open the door, see us playing, and laugh.

Algernon would go for frequent checkups to monitor and adjust the medication he was taking for his IBD and to deal with occasional flare-ups when he couldn't keep his food down and had to stay overnight to get fluids and medication intravenously. All the vet techs, as well as our general practice veterinarian and the veterinary internist, talked about how friendly he was.

He played chair-basketball with me at every visit until he suddenly went blind. Every night of my life with Ernest and Algernon, I knew which cat was sitting on my chest without turning on the light. When one of them got up to eat in the middle of the night, I could tell who it was because each cat made a different chewing sound. If I had gone blind instead of Algernon, I would have been completely aware of who was purring in my ear or licking my face. Although cats with IBD are susceptible to cancer, Algernon didn't show any signs of it, so the veterinary neurologist who examined him thought he had an infection that could be treated with medication. His sight was unlikely to return, but cats rely more on their other senses. Algernon learned to navigate around our apartment and would clamber onto the armchair in the living room, where he'd spend the afternoon napping with his legs tangled around Ernest while I worked at my desk.

The morning Algernon fell over on his side and couldn't get up, I took him to the hospital before driving to my teaching job, which was an hour away. My class didn't meet until evening, but I had appointments throughout the day. He seemed to be feeling better when I dropped him off, so I planned to visit him—maybe even take him home—after class that night. Algernon clung to me when the technician tried to take him inside to the inpatient area, and as I unwrapped his paws from around my neck, I'm sure I sounded scolding and dismissive, as though he had nothing to worry about and shouldn't be so scared of being handed over to a stranger who would put him into a cage in a room full of sick animals. When I got a call from the hospital that Algernon had taken a turn for the worse, I canceled my class and headed back.

Algernon's body had begun to shut down. But his will to live was so great that he fooled me—and probably himself too—into believing that he would be with me for years to come as a wise, blind cat. It was the first day of the Cherry Blossom Festival. A long line of cars was trying to get into the city, and I was stuck in traffic on the Theodore Roosevelt Bridge when the veterinarian called for the last time. I never got to say goodbye to Algernon because I didn't believe he was dying.

Grief is personal and generic at once. Each instance is so different and yet exactly the same, like the view from the bridge where I was stopped—the Washington Monument ahead, the Lincoln Memorial off to the side—familiar yet unreal: one of those sights I knew by heart long before I experienced the real thing. It was no use being told that I had done the best I could for him. I didn't care whether or not that was true. I had wanted him to live forever and, failing that, to die only when and where I could assure him that I had not abandoned him.

I couldn't help but go over the bad decisions I had made all day. My apartment was ten minutes from the animal hospital. If I had faced the seriousness of the situation and stayed home, I could have been there in time for him to have at least heard my voice, among all the ones he didn't know, trying to help him in ways he couldn't possibly understand. Instead, I had handed him over. The last thing I said was a promise I couldn't keep: "Don't worry. I'll be back after school."

When I finally arrived at the animal hospital that April evening, Gail was waiting for me. I had called her from the road. The two of us sat in the examination room with Algernon's body and cried. She talked me into requesting the individual cremation for his remains. With her at my side, I didn't have to be overwhelmed by grief and confusion, the way I was when Oscar died in Cambridge.

Ernest was waiting by the door when I came home from the animal hospital empty-handed. He was used to Algernon being gone for a few days to be treated for his flare-ups, so he might not have figured out right away that his brother was not coming back. I'd heard of cats that went around the house looking for their companions, or those who behaved in an especially clingy way after a companion's death. Ernest had no reason to do either of these things since he and Algernon had never hidden from each other. Besides, our small apartment didn't have many places to hide, and alone or together with Algernon, Ernest had always followed me around the apartment. If he was being especially needy, I didn't notice. It was more that I clung to him and became reluctant to leave the house. In the next weeks, the two of us spent long evenings watching TV in bed. Around two or three in the morning, we'd simply go from sitting up to lying down.

After her more outgoing cat, Hokey, died, my neighbor Kirsten noticed the other cat, Blacksburg, moving up a few inches every night from the foot of the bed, where he used to sleep, until he finally claimed the spot Hokey had occupied next to her head. But Ernest continued to sleep fully stretched over my legs and stomach, on top of the bedcovers, his long body like an extra blanket pinning me down. I never figured out if he didn't move because that was his favorite spot already or because he was honoring Algernon's place under the covers next to me. Ernest completely immobilized my legs and torso, but my arms, which used to be wrapped around Algernon, were now free to move. I often woke up with my hand cupping Ernest's head, which rested on my solar plexus, the point from which a complex nervous system radiates. We were fused together, grief flowing quietly back and forth between us.

The day after Algernon died, a woman from the crematorium called to direct me to their website so I could choose a box for his ashes. I was relieved to be alone, at home, to view the pictures of the tiny decorative boxes, which were ridiculous and pitiful and oddly moving at once. When the box was delivered to the animal hospital along with the paw print the woman at the crematorium had taken before the cremation, Gail offered to pick them up.

The wooden box was dark brown, with a gold ribbon and silk flowers. I put it on the shelf in the foyer next to Algernon's picture. Gail made me a drink, and we unpacked the small cardboard box containing the clay paw print. The round disk, wrapped in plastic, had four sharp indentations where Algernon's claws had gone in. It was accompanied by instructions for decorating it further (with the pet's name or stenciled flowers) and then baking it in the oven to set the print. In the decades I'd been baking, I had never burned anything, but at that moment, all I could think of was the batch of cream puff shells that my seventh-grade home economics class had turned into lava rocks. It didn't help that the disk was almost exactly the same size as a sugar cookie.

"Gail, I just can't," I said.

"Don't worry," she said. "I can."

Gail worked as a collections manager at the American Indian Museum and handled fragile objects every day. She applied gold leaf to the disk for Algernon and found a small wooden stand to put it on.

My book about knitting was published two months before Algernon died. With no new project in mind, I would have been content to spend the summer lounging on the couch with the cats in my lap, reading and jotting down ideas in my journal, resting and recharging for whatever came next. To have everything in one place—work, rest, solitude, community—had been the goal of my journey with Ernest and Algernon, who had rescued me from the empty silence after Oscar's death. But now once again, I was sitting at my desk with no thoughts worth writing about. Often, I looked up from the book in my hands and couldn't remember what I had just read. As always, Ernest was on me all the time. But now our closeness felt sad and airless.

One Saturday evening in late April, almost a month after Algernon's death, I gathered a dozen friends in my apartment. With New Orleans-style jazz blaring out of a portable speaker, we danced under the shelf where I had placed Algernon's ashes, then marched out the door, down the hallways, and around the grounds outside. Some of us were waving white handkerchiefs; others were swinging fishpole-style cat toys with feathers.

"I didn't know how else to get unstuck," I told my friends, as though our collective physical movement could push me out of my sadness. Having friends who humored and supported me was a consolation, but when they were gone, Ernest and I would still be alone in our quiet apartment. We needed something more than a ritual, and everyone knew it.

"I hope you're ready to be a big brother again," I told Ernest after the guests left and he jumped down from his perch into my lap.

A week later, I took him in for a complete physical. All the tests came back showing that his IBD was under control and he was otherwise in excellent health. The veterinarian agreed that the next few months would be the perfect time for him to get used to a new companion.

Chapter Ten

Ernest and Miles

The purple clusters of mountain laurel blossoms lined the walkway of the large log-style home in the woods outside St. Mary's City, Maryland. Inside the house, the hardwood floor on the main level was spotless. In the basement and also on the second floor, pregnant and nursing cats were set up, each in her own room. Visitors were asked to cleanse their hands with disinfectant wipes before entering a new area.

A petite woman in her thirties with brown hair cut straight across her nape, Heather, who owned the house, resembled a Siamese cat herself. I had come with Gail to the spring open house at her cattery because of the photograph on her website showing a newborn kitten held in her husband's palm.

"We start socializing our kittens from the moment they are born," the caption read.

Conditioning cats to trust humans is not difficult, but it has a narrow window of opportunity. Kittens who are handled within seven weeks of being born will remain friendlier for life than those who only receive contact after that. Heather said she made a point of holding and playing with each kitten every day. Since Siamese cats, as a breed, are curious and outgoing, the early contact she provided doubly ensured their friendliness. The eight-week-old kittens in the playroom came up to Gail and me and crawled all over us. You could pick them up, put them on the floor, turn them over onto their backs, touch them on their stomachs, tug at their tails, rub their heads, and stroke their ears, and they would keep purring and headbutting you. All the available kittens were reserved for other people, but Heather was expecting more soon.

Cat and Bird

I gave her a deposit to reserve a kitten and filled out the preference form. All the cats of my life had been male, and so had the majority of the really friendly cats I'd met at other people's houses. So I checked the boxes for "male" and "any color." In the blank space left for "other comments," I scribbled, "I would like a particularly affectionate individual—demanding and clingy."

In June, Heather sent me a photograph of a kitten looking straight at the camera with pale blue eyes, his left front paw hooked over a rubber ball as though he was getting in position to lob it for a winning shot. This kitten, a male blue-point, would be weaned and fully vaccinated in early July. Heather said I could meet him first, but I told her I would just come and pick him up whenever he was ready. In the picture—which was a formal portrait, no less—the kitten looked amazingly confident and purposeful. At six weeks old, he was already a cat who knew his own character and potential.

I decided to name him after Miles Davis because the kitten was "kind of blue." Also because, if a Siamese cat were to play a musical instrument, it would surely be the trumpet.

Dorian and I had listened repeatedly to another Miles Davis album, *Sketches of Spain*, as I unpacked my boxes in the writing studio in Wisconsin after we had moved there to live. Almost twenty years later, the era of Oscar Wilde cats was over because I couldn't think of another good name from one of his works. But the legacy could go on with strains that were at once familiar and different, like Miles Davis replaying flamenco with jazz variations.

Miles and I met in the parking lot of a natural healing center a few miles outside St. Mary's City. It was eight o'clock on a Saturday morning. Heather had chosen the parking lot because the huge rainbow-colored sign advertising "Massage, Acupuncture, Herbal Medicine" was easy to spot from the highway. She opened the back hatch of her SUV and transferred the kitten from her pet carrier to mine. As I reached out to take my carrier, which looked like a gym bag, Miles saw me through its mesh top and turned over on his back. His stomach was hairless and pink. The contract said that the moment the kitten was in my possession, he was entirely my responsibility, so I resisted the urge to unzip the bag and touch him. I imagined him wiggling out from under my hand, jumping out of the bag, and dashing across the parking lot. Miles didn't know me yet and had no reason to want to stay.

I gave Heather a cashier's check, we shook hands, and I started walking toward Gail's red Honda CR-V (which she thereafter called the "Cat Retrieval Vehicle"). Inside the bag, Miles was rolling around on his back, alternately purring and meowing. He was getting louder and louder.

"You said you wanted a clingy cat," Heather called after me. "Well, you got one."

Once we were in the car with the door closed, I unzipped the carrier just enough to put my hand inside. Miles was still on his back. My hand covered his entire body. His stomach was soft and warm, and I could feel his chest vibrating as he continued to purr. He wasn't going to run away from me, now or ever. Gail wouldn't have minded if I'd taken him out and held him, but ever since my near-fiasco on the freeway with Oscar years earlier, I'd adhered to a strict policy about cats staying in their carriers in any moving vehicle.

Miles—who would grow up to be pale gray, kind of blue, with shadowy ripples of lynx-point stripes—closed his eyes, arched his back, and stretched his legs while I rubbed his chest and stomach. When I stopped, he meowed in protest. "Me, me, me," he wailed in a loud, high-pitched voice like a cicada's.

Cat and Bird

I removed my hand and closed the bag. Miles sprang to his feet and reached with his front paw to jab at the mesh top. He had a boxer's stance, alert and combative. Each of us had sized up the situation and was trying to decide how we should start training the other. I unzipped the carrier partway and put my hand back inside. Miles pressed his chest to my palm and began purring again. Great, I thought as he turned over on his back and wrapped his legs around my wrist. It's you. You're finally here.

Following the advice of cat behavior books, I let Ernest and Miles get used to each other's smells and voices and fed them on opposite sides of a closed door. They were sitting together on the couch by the end of the second day. I sent around a picture, and one of my neighbors wrote back, "Your Next Project: World Peace." From that night on, the two cats slept with me, Ernest in his usual spot on my legs and Miles on my chest. During the day, they played, groomed each other, and sat together on the couch or the cat perch. Miles looked like Ernest's miniature, his "mini-me" as one friend put it. It was the best start I could have hoped for; Ernest took charge of the kitten with great confidence and playfulness.

But on the ninth night after Miles's arrival, after the two cats had been running around the apartment and batting at each other all day, Ernest began throwing up. I assumed it was the result of jumping on top of the fridge—where I thought he was too heavy to go—to eat the kitten food I was giving to Miles. I took him to the animal hospital, where he was in and out over the next several days. Each time I left the apartment with him and returned home alone, Miles would come to the door, lie down on the floor, and wait for me to pick him up.

After three days of throwing up, coughing, and refusing to eat, Ernest was finally placed in an oxygen tent. The technician would turn up the oxygen when I visited so I could unzip the nylon tent and put my head and hand inside. Ernest was alert enough to press his head against my hand. I petted him and told him that I wanted him to get better. I also knew he'd be miserable if he had to linger and shuttle between specialty clinics.

"If you can't," I managed to say, "I'll understand. I'll always love you."

The test results showed that he had pancreatitis and a lung infection. I left to let him rest and receive antibiotics through an IV. A few minutes after I got home, the veterinarian called to say that Ernest had died. Once again, if I had stayed a little longer, I could have been with him at the end. Once again, I had walked away as if the situation weren't already a crisis and I would have another chance. Ernest's death was even more sudden than Algernon's, and once again, Gail was there to do all the things of which I was incapable: the ribboned wooden box, the gold-leafed paw print.

Pancreatitis is an incurable disease in which a cat's pancreas begins to destroy itself. Miles sneezed now and then as most kittens do, but all the veterinarians who'd examined him assured me that Ernest's death wasn't caused by the new kitten's arrival. Ernest's lung infection was a result of his weakened immune system. Still, the coincidence nagged at me, as though he'd been waiting for me to get another cat so he could pass me on to his successor and make the quickest exit possible.

My mind was empty and yet cluttered, like a building flattened by a tornado. I wouldn't have known how to start sorting through the destruction if it hadn't been for Miles demanding my attention. I wondered if he found it confusing to have lived with Ernest for such a short time. But Miles had grown up in a cattery. Every week, new kittens were born, weaned, and sent away. He had been separated from his mother, his litter mates, and his original human caretakers and handed over to me in a parking lot. Now, with Ernest gone, he was alone in a new home with no one but me, a confused, grieving human, and Miles became the focal point around which everything—including my grief for Ernest and Algernon—fell into place. It was a lot to ask of a cat; luckily, he was born and bred for the job.

In the subsequent weeks, Miles and I quickly learned how to take care of each other through this time of transition. A former student gave me a set of stylish stainless-steel bowls, originally meant for humans, that she said were rated as the best bowls ever for dry cat food. I filled them four times a day with kitten food whose ingredients included minerals, vitamins, and "clinically proven antioxidants for immune support." All the specialty formulas I had tried hadn't kept Ernest and Algernon from dying young, but I couldn't give up on my search for the perfect food on which to raise a healthy kitten.

During the day, Miles would follow me around the apartment and sit in my lap while I wrote at my desk, read on the couch, ate dinner on the living room floor, and watched TV in bed. At night, he alternated between sleeping on my legs the way Ernest did and crawling under the covers into my arms, taking Algernon's spot.

My next-door neighbor, a violinist with very sensitive hearing, was not a pet person, so I decided that Miles should sleep through the night instead of meowing and running around before dawn the way all my other cats did as kittens. So at bedtime, we had a long play session, followed by me feeding him his largest meal of the day. Hunt, eat, groom, and sleep. It wasn't difficult to calibrate his internal clock to mine, though I was equally adjusting mine to his.

I didn't feel like socializing, but everyone wanted to see the new kitten. My friends brought us rubber balls, mice and birds made of feathers and felt, chewy nylon fabrics twisted into pretzels. Miles would bat these toys around until they ended up under the furniture. Sometimes he'd come running to me with a felt mouse or a nylon pretzel and drop it at my feet. Like all my cats, he played fetch in an unorganized, desultory manner. He brought me a toy and continued to retrieve it until stashing it somewhere. He would fetch five or six times but only if he brought me the toy first. When I tried to initiate the game by showing him a toy and then throwing it, he would run to it, pick it up in his mouth, and promptly put it in his food bowl. Dorian used to do the same thing, though he chose his water bowl, so the toys always got soaked.

Miles's favorite interactive toy was a mouse made of bristle that was attached to a plastic wand with flexible wire. The idea was for me to dangle the artificial prey in front of him and make him chase it, but his version of the game didn't emphasize the pursuit. He caught the mouse easily, held it in his mouth like a bit, and walked me around the apartment. Although he was growing fast, he weighed just under three pounds, and his markings were still very faint. He looked like a miniature white pony leading his handler around the circus ring. School was out for the summer. Every day I read, wrote, and walked in circles with Miles, as though the two of us were tracing the big hole in the world left by Ernest.

Cat and Bird

In memory of Ernest, my friend Stephen helped me install a platform-style bird feeder in the window next to my desk. It's a simple rectangular tray, twelve by eight inches, with a mesh bottom. The tray had to be secured so it would not tip over when birds landed on it and crash to the walkway below. The metal screws that came with the feeder didn't work on a window ledge made of concrete, so Stephen devised a board with brackets to hold the tray and anchored the board behind a planter filled with rocks. The arrangement elevated the feeder above the clay planter and made it look almost like an altar.

A few days later, a blue jay alighted on the window ledge to eat from it for the first time. The other regulars were catbirds, house sparrows, house finches, mourning doves, cardinals, goldfinches, chickadees, Carolina wrens, downy woodpeckers, hairy woodpeckers, white-breasted nuthatches, red-bellied woodpeckers, and tufted titmice, the tiny, mouse-colored birds that had visited Oscar and me in Boston. In Washington, tufted titmice and a few other species that only summered in Massachusetts and Wisconsin were year-round residents. I had never been able to see so many songbirds without leaving my house, but Miles scarcely noticed them.

Among the few birds that were abundant in the area but never at my window were robins, the only birds Ernest had ever watched with interest. Robins are not seed-eaters, so they aren't attracted to bird feeders, and my window on the third floor was too high to watch them foraging on the ground. As I observed the daily drama of bird life—the pair of cardinals at dawn, the doves jockeying for position at dusk—the absence of the robins was the silence around Ernest's demise. Outside our window, wings continued to beat against gravity. Feathers and hollow bones rose into the air. But now, in Ernest's place, I was the only one keeping watch.

Chapter Eleven

Pet Grief

The superstition about cats having nine lives started in the Middle Ages, after Pope Gregory XI declared cats to be servants of Satan. Their ability to survive falls and elude capture was taken as proof of their protection by the devil. In reality, the average life span of an indoor cat is fourteen years, compared to a human's seventy-seven years in America. Humans are the ones with multiple cat lives, left alone to grieve each fragile life span.

I had made my friends march around our building after Algernon's death, hoping to mobilize myself out of grief, and it had worked long enough to summon Miles to my side. But then Ernest died, and I found myself crying in my car every time I had to cross the Theodore Roosevelt Bridge on my way home from work, overlooking the Tidal Basin and imagining the cherry blossoms at sunset because my memory got stuck on the April evening Algernon died, even though we were now in a completely different season and the lanes were dark and empty. With both Ernest and Algernon gone, I was barely clinging to my fifth cat life with Miles.

I had never before found myself crying about the same thing again and again. It didn't usually take me six months to see that my situation wasn't so bad compared to other people's problems or for me to move on to some new preoccupation of my own. I had cried after Dorian and Oscar died too, but each of them had been sick for a couple of months with no hope of recovery, so the end was not a surprise. Losing Algernon and Ernest so quickly together had stunned me. Talking to friends was only making me sadder instead of giving me a sense of perspective and solidarity. I needed help from a trained professional who knew how to guide strangers through their loss.

Support groups for people who have lost their pets didn't exist until 1982, when upwards of sixty people met every month at the Animal Medical Center in Manhattan to talk about their pets and share pictures of them. Soon, animal hospitals and humane shelters across the country formed similar groups of their own. By 2010, the year Ernest and Algernon died, pet-owners' grief, or "pet grief" as it came to be known, had a national website that provided state-by-state listings of counseling services and support groups.

One of those groups met at an animal shelter in Fairfax, Virginia—the city in which my university was located—every third Wednesday of the month. According to the website, the group's leader had conducted grief-counseling workshops around the country and had appeared on numerous television news programs. I tried to envision the meeting, but the only images I had of support groups came from TV shows like *The Wire* and *The Sopranos*, which portrayed seriously disturbed people who were engaged in substance abuse and murder. They sat in a circle in a windowless room, confiding in each other about burying bodies at construction sites and selling drugs to children. But Fairfax was not Baltimore or Newark. Surely, suburban pet owners in Northern Virginia were people whose stories could shed light on mine.

The website for the Fairfax support group emphasized the importance of participants sharing their stories, but I didn't expect anyone, including the counselor, to hear me talk about Ernest and Algernon and offer tips for overcoming my grief. A support group, I surmised, was intended to offer a peer-learning opportunity, much like a creative writing workshop. As a professor, I always started the semester by telling my students that they would learn more from discussing their classmates' work than from having theirs discussed. The purpose of the class was not to give them useful advice but to leave them with questions that might, over time, lead to deeper understanding. Instead of looking for immediate answers, the students had to stay patient and open-minded, cultivating their ability to give constructive criticism. To learn something from the people I was about to meet, I too needed to have the right combination of respect and skepticism, honesty and restraint.

My Wednesday class ended at 7:00 p.m. At 7:30, the meeting's start time, I arrived at the animal shelter's one-story building with a chain-link fence in the back. Two other cars were parked in the lot, and a woman in a beige suit with a knee-length skirt was getting out of one of them. I caught up with her outside the door.

"Are you here for the pet loss meeting?" she asked me. A thin woman in her sixties, she had the wan appearance of a smoker and a voice to match. Her platinum blond hair was cut close to her face, emphasizing her cheekbones.

"Yes," I nodded.

"Welcome," she said. "I'm Caroline. I lead the group." While I was shaking her hand, she reached out with the other to press the buzzer on the security box. "Hey, it's Caroline," she barked into the intercom.

A young woman in a navy-blue uniform opened the door and then walked to the only other car parked in the lot and drove away. The building was dark save for the florescent light above the now unattended desk. The animals waiting to be adopted must have been behind a locked door or in another building because I heard no barking, meowing, shuffling, or clicking of toenails as I followed Caroline down a narrow hallway into a room with yellow linoleum; it was twice the size of the classroom I had just come from. She turned on the light and pointed to the black plastic chairs stacked against the wall.

"Do you mind setting the chairs in a circle? I should go and watch the door."

"How many chairs do we need?"

"Maybe twelve? You never know with this group."

The door buzzer went off as I was completing the circle. Caroline returned with a heavyset woman in a flannel shirt, a gray button-down sweater, and baggy jeans. The woman's attire was as pointedly frumpy as Caroline's suit was businesslike. In my long black coat, black dress, and tall boots, my hair pulled back in a ponytail, I also looked like a parody of myself: an aging hippie academic. Caroline seated herself in one of the chairs, and the other woman settled next to her. I heard no other voices or footsteps in the hallway. If more people were expected, Caroline would be watching the door. I dropped my backpack to the floor, sat down, and realized I was seated on the other side of the circle. We were like characters in a one-act play.

"Let's get started," Caroline said, nodding to the other woman before addressing me across the empty circle. "This is Nancy. She's been in this group for a few years, and now she comes to help me with the program."

"I lost my favorite dog three years ago and this group saved my life," Nancy explained. She had a wide, serene face and shoulder-length, salt-and-pepper hair. "I come back to help other people in the same boat."

"Why don't you start the meeting," Caroline said to me, "by explaining why you're here?"

The room was quiet. Nothing like this had happened to me

since my senior year in college, when I went to my American literature class—which had only five students—the morning after a big campus party. The professor waited ten minutes for the others to show up, then canceled the class when they didn't. I had a feeling I wouldn't be getting the same break now. So I talked about Algernon dying in April and Ernest in July.

Caroline asked me if this was the first time I'd lost pets. I shook my head and told her about Dorian and Oscar. She gasped when I said Oscar died at three.

"No wonder you're feeling so terrible," she said. "You've lost your two cats while you were still mourning the loss of your last cat. And now you have this new kitten at home, and that must be so confusing. I'm going to ask Nancy to tell her story. You might find some help in it."

Nancy plunged into her anecdotes without providing any background information, but in time, I figured out that she was married, that she and her husband owned two houses, and that they traveled between the houses with their three white Maltese terriers. Her favorite, Butchie, died three years ago.

"My most important advice to you is *write everything down*," she said. "You always think you'll remember, but you won't. I have notebooks all over my houses. Whenever I remember something about Butchie, I jot it down."

The conundrum of grief is the same for pets as it is for people: how can we remember the dead, how can we not leave them behind when every moment propels us further away from the past we shared with them? The only way I could keep my mother in my life was to survive her death and become a writer. So I should have known that when Nancy jotted down memories of Butchie, she was securing her hold on their years together. By making a note at the very instant the memory occurred, she was sewing the present into the past, like a needle and thread looping back half a stitch before piercing through to the other side and reappearing a full stitch forward. Each notebook was a quilted blanket with countless backstitches to fasten all the layers of her life in place. No wonder she found solace in having dozens of notebooks scattered around her two houses. But as I sat in the hard chair on the other side of the circle, I felt overwhelmed by the mere idea of all those stacked notebooks: all those hundreds, thousands of words, perhaps immobilizing rather than propelling her forward. I wondered if my writing, too, was an excuse not to live in the present. The past, however flawed, was familiar ground. The temptation to stay there, looking for words, more words, was almost irresistible. At its core, grief was oddly comforting.

"Some people find it helpful to write a letter to their pets," Caroline interjected, "especially if they didn't get to say goodbye. It's never too late to perform a ritual of letting go." She said I should accept that my cats were never coming back, let go of any anger I felt toward them for dying and leaving me alone, and know that it was not unusual for people to be grief-stricken for months, even years. "You've lost so much," she said, finally.

Then she asked Nancy to talk about her spiritual experience.

"I'm not one of those New Age-y people," Nancy began. "I'm a very practical person. I was surprised by what happened to me."

Apparently, a few months after Butchie's death, she started seeing blue and yellow butterflies in her garden. Butchie had worn a blue collar, and yellow was Nancy's favorite color. She had never noticed butterflies like these before. But now they were appearing among her flowers whenever she thought about him. "So I asked an animal communicator, who had come to help me with one of my dogs who has arthritis, to tell Butchie how much I really appreciated the butterflies, but I wanted more signs that he was okay. She said that three more signs would come to me."

A week later, Nancy heard a dog barking in the special way that only Butchie barked. Then, one summer evening at dusk, she saw a Maltese standing on the other side of her pool. Her three dogs were next to her, and there wasn't another Maltese in the neighborhood, so the dog she saw could only be Butchie. Then on Thanksgiving, she was in the kitchen holding a large bowl of salad when she felt a dog bump her leg and push his head against her knee. Her three dogs were sleeping next to the fireplace. She could still feel the dog's weight against her leg, but she couldn't see under the bowl. As she slowly lowered the bowl to the kitchen table, the invisible dog pressed his head against her leg even harder, then the weight suddenly lifted and he was gone. The other dogs continued to sleep. None of them had stirred in the few minutes that Butchie had been with her.

"So now I know Butchie is okay," she said flatly.

An animal communicator is someone who claims to understand your pets, dead or alive, through psychic powers, and can possibly bring them momentarily back from the dead. Nancy believed that this stranger with no veterinary training could tell her more about her dog's arthritis than she could from observing him daily.

Of course, I too longed to feel Ernest and Algernon's heads pressing against my knee one more time, but asking for a sign they were "okay" was delusional. They were not okay and would never be again—that's what it means to die. In fact, Algernon was already not okay when I last saw him; he was near death when I dropped him off at the hospital and rushed off to work. By pretending otherwise, I had belittled and betrayed him. No ritual could change that now. To write him a farewell letter to make myself feel better would only be an added insult.

"Some people believe our pets are still with us," Caroline said, "while others believe only humans have souls, so our pets are just *gone* when they die." She paused, presumably waiting for my response.

Although I didn't believe in God, I hadn't completely ruled out the possibility that the dead were still with us in some abstract, molecular form, no longer themselves but still present as a form of energy. I certainly didn't think that only humans had an afterlife and our pets just died. I could have emphasized our common ground, but the way Caroline had presented the two options—either our pets are still with us or only humans have souls—left no room for discussion. As I looked across the empty circle at Caroline, I felt a sudden irritation.

"It's arrogant to assume that humans continue to exist after death and animals don't," I said. "We can't be that special."

Caroline smiled and nodded in encouragement.

"Actually, I'm pretty sure that we all cease to exist," I continued. "When we die, we're gone, we become nothing. I'm not afraid of being nothing after I die since I was nothing before I was born. I don't believe my dead cats are still around. I don't expect to be around, myself, after I die. We go from an eternity of not existing to another eternity of not existing. I have no desire to linger around for eternity; to continue forever as myself—a limited being in the infinite universe— feels like a punishment."

Caroline sat up straighter and didn't say anything for a long time. When she recovered her speech, she said, "If that's your view, then grief is going to be very different for you."

Different from what? I wondered.

Just about every religion on earth offers its believers a reassuring vision of heaven or paradise, but all we can say for certain is that after our death, we will no longer be who we once were or have the same thoughts, feelings, or desires. Surely, that is the biggest heartbreak of all. Caroline must have encountered agnostics or atheists in her work as a counselor before. People who didn't believe in God or an afterlife had pets and grieved for them too. But maybe they—we—didn't go to support groups because opening up to strangers required the most arduous faith of all: trust. And even though I truly believed what I had told her, I knew too that I was failing miserably at the task I had set out to accomplish: to keep an open mind. I didn't have the right balance of respect and skepticism, honesty and restraint, after all. From the moment I sat down in the circle, I'd been passing judgment on everything Caroline and Nancy said. It had been my choice to come here, to seek help, but I really only wanted to be left alone.

Caroline proceeded to recap her advice—write everything down, perform a ritual, accept that the cats are never coming back, let go of your anger, know that overcoming grief takes time—but now it all echoed with her repeated disclaimer: "Grief is going to be very different for you."

Her original assumption that I believed in God or the afterlife wasn't unusual: almost everyone made that conjecture about everyone else and dispensed advice accordingly. And now she was stumped because it's nearly impossible to devise a ritual without religious overtones. In truth, if she had told me to burn incense in front of Algernon's picture every night and meditate on our life together, I wouldn't have done it, but I wouldn't have been so upset.

What I really resented wasn't the religious assumption but the equally naive notion that writing can lead to "closure."

Cat and Bird

Composing a farewell letter for my own peace of mind would not only belittle Algernon but also violate the faith I had in the act of writing itself. Writing wasn't a simple task with a practical purpose. For me, it was the only way of revealing the truth: a long meandering path with no guarantees. My letter to Algernon would most likely remain unfinished for years, and if I ever completed it to my satisfaction, the result wouldn't be entirely consoling. Any truth I discovered would embody all the things that make up an elegy—regret, sorrow, fear for my own mortality—since that is what a proper letter to Algernon would have to be.

At the end of the session, Caroline handed me a brochure that featured "Rainbow Bridge," a story about a green meadow located on "this side of Heaven," where all the pets who died can "run and play together" while they wait for us to join them. The story claims that after we cross the bridge into heaven, we will then be reunited with our beloved animals, never to be parted again. Most resources about pet grief feature this story and show the same picture of a rainbow connecting two puffy white clouds, an image which can also be purchased as an accessory—a porcelain pin, for example.

My main objection to "Rainbow Bridge" isn't its commercial use and religious overtones or its appalling purple prose. It's that whoever wrote the story obviously knew nothing about house cats. Ernest and Algernon were always indoors. Even if they could get used to being outside in the afterlife, they wouldn't want to "frolic" in a meadow with millions of other cats, dogs, birds, rabbits, iguanas, and a host of pocket pets that they wouldn't be able to chase, capture, and, ideally, eat. If I needed a story to help me accept the deaths of my cats and my grief about them, I would have to write my own.

Outside the shelter's door, I thanked Caroline for the meeting, and we parted ways.

"You know, you're doing really well," Nancy said as we crossed the lot toward our cars, parked side by side. "Most people who come to this meeting can't sleep or eat. They have a hard time keeping their jobs. It was like that for me."

Her eyes looked sad. She was trying to be kind. I should have apologized for my earlier comments. To insist that we all become nothing was to say that her three signs were meaningless. I should have said that I respected her faith. Only it wouldn't have been true.

Unlike the people she was referring to, including herself, I didn't struggle with my daily routine. I lacked the willpower to stop eating and sleeping altogether or to miss a class or an appointment, knowing that people were waiting and depending on me. The last thing I wanted when I was feeling low was the chaos and drama that came with neglecting my job or showing up in public looking disheveled and distraught. Maintaining basic self-care was the path of least resistance. Like the orphaned nestlings who opened their mouths when a syringe of food appeared in front of them, I never questioned my need to live. I didn't have lethally disturbing thoughts like my mother when she sat alone in our new house. The stuff inside my head was amorphous, an endless loop of vague impressions. Being sequestered with it all day long turned me into a feeble, washed-out imitation of who I am: not a threat to myself or a burden to others.

So I thanked Nancy again, got into my car, and drove off.

But then, shortly after I attended that support group, I too began writing down memories of my cats. My ultimate goal, however, was not to write everything down but the opposite.

Cat and Bird

I longed to reshape my myriad recollections into a few words, just the right words, distilling the chaotic abundance of "real life" into a single narrative I could shelter on the page. Then and only then would I be able to remember and forget at once, for always.

Chapter Twelve

Miles and Jackson

Miles was always waiting at the door when I came home from school. Like Dorian, he'd bump into me and fall over at my feet. Or he'd jump from the floor to my shoulder as Oscar used to do, clinging to my neck, and we'd walk around the apartment with him perched on my shoulder like a parrot. After going around two or three times, I would stop in the living room and slowly lean forward until he hopped off my shoulder onto the couch. He then followed me while I put away my jacket, books, and papers, and as soon as I sat down on the floor to take off my shoes, he would start circling me again.

Miles didn't leave my side to saunter around the apartment. He walked in tighter and tighter circles, bumping my legs, shoulders, and arms with his head, taking a few steps, leaning sideways to press his whole body against mine, then reaching up to rub our cheeks together. He'd arch his back to be petted, purr loudly, plop down on the floor, extend his legs, and roll over on his back. He'd rock from side to side, his whiskers trembling, while I scratched his stomach. The moment I stopped, he'd get up and resume winding himself around me, pressing his head against me every few steps, enclosing me in the countless circles he drew around me every day. He was casting a spell to keep me from leaving his side and disappearing.

People in the Middle Ages believed that witches slipped into the bodies of their cats to roam around spying on their neighbors, making them sick. I half believed that Miles and I shared one body, though he never left my side to do anything devious or useful. He was on me around the clock, asleep in my arms, curled up in my lap, wrapped around my neck, or perched on the desk, our shoulders touching, to supervise my writing. Whenever I needed him to nap alone so I could cook on the stove or work with yarn—activities I didn't consider safe for him—I unwrapped his paws from around my neck and carefully positioned him on the blanket on the couch as though he was a detachable part of myself, like a battery taken out to be recharged.

"You sleep and rest for me," I said. "I need to do this one thing without you."

Every time he coughed or threw up—two things most kittens do regularly—I got choked up and sick to my stomach. He was all I thought about, and yet he kept meowing and circling and watching to make sure I wasn't going to abandon him. Being with Ernest after Algernon's death, and now with Miles after losing Ernest, I couldn't separate love from worry. Animal companionship was its own turbulent weather system. With Miles, I was back at sea, the two of us huddled on a flimsy sailboat spinning in the eye of a hurricane.

I remembered how my grandmother opened all the windows in her house after thunderstorms and moved houseplants, teapots, vases, hairbrushes, and other small objects out of the way to clear the path for any evil spirit to leave the house. She was careful where she placed mirrors on the wall and furniture around the house to ensure the proper path of energy from room to room. Although she didn't have a name for what to her was common sense, she was following *feng shui*, the Chinese practice that would become popular in the 1980s among my American friends.

My home could have used a better energy flow, but I wasn't interested in rearranging the furniture. Only a new cat could redirect the whirlwind of anxiety in which Miles and I were trapped. We needed a kitten who was affectionate but calm, an animal immune to anxiety. If I could get an easygoing cat to balance Miles's nervous disposition, the three of us could steer ourselves back to the calm lake I imagined boating across with Ernest and Algernon. And with luck, we could float around in peace much longer than I had with them.

The one thing I didn't worry about was how Miles would get along with another kitten because the biggest mystery of domestic cats as a species is their sociability. Only a few big cats in the wild, like lions, hunt together and raise their young in family groups. The African wildcat, the house cat's direct ancestor, spends most of its life completely alone, each female occupying an area of about five hundred acres and defending it from intrusion by other females. Males and females meet only to mate; and the young, at four or five months of age, disperse, leaving their mother to resume her solitary life.

Modern house cats, by contrast, can reside in pairs and trios inside a small apartment or share a playroom at a shelter or a cat café with a dozen others. Even feral cats often live in colonies, coexisting amicably in barns or parks so long as there is an adequate supply of food. "Live and let live" is the least you can expect from multiple felines in the same household: they can each have a separate relationship with the human caretaker and "get along" in the superficial way my brother and I did in our childhood. Too different to come together even to fight, Jumpei and I coexisted by ignoring each other. But I wanted Miles and his companion to be complements rather than opposites. Ernest and Algernon had been a perfect pair, but this time, I didn't think another Siamese would be a good choice.

Siamese cats are known for their intense, obsessive, and stubborn nature. Their strong devotion to their owner is an expression of their overall monomaniacal tendencies. Dorian attacked all my friends, and Ernest refused to make himself at home for an entire year in Milwaukee. Oscar and Algernon used their singular focus in a more constructive manner, Oscar by being so eager to make a home anywhere and Algernon in the fierce will he showed to continue living even when his health began to decline. Of all my cats, Algernon was the only one who could be described as easygoing, but after we were settled in Washington, DC, even he started taking instant, inexplicable dislikes toward a few people he perceived as intruders: he bit the cat-sitter I hired when all my neighbors were out of town and scratched one of my colleagues when she sat down next to him on the couch in the middle of a party, after several other guests had held and petted him with great mutual enjoyment.

At five months old, Miles had practically sewn himself to my side. On the few occasions when I was in the building's hallway but not coming in—because I was chatting with a neighbor or unpacking boxes I didn't want to bring inside (Miles chewed cardboard)—he would pick up one of his toys and pace around the apartment, carrying it and meowing with his mouth full. When I came in, he would drop the toy at my feet but refuse to fetch if I threw it. The noise he made with his mouth full was loud and distorted, a clear distress call. Miles had a double dose of every Siamese quality. If I wanted a relaxed cat to improve the feline *feng shui* of our home, I needed to consider another breed.

One of my "guilty pleasure" readings over the years had been *Cat Fancy* magazine, a monthly publication about cat shows, feline health, product reviews, human interest stories involving cats, and a state-by-state directory of breeders. Every issue featured a "breed profile" with the grand champion from that breed photographed on the cover like a movie star on celebrity magazines. I became interested in Bombay cats after reading about them in the magazine. Bombays were copper-eyed black cats bred in the United States. They resembled miniature panthers, but unlike Savannah and Bengal cats, the truly exotic breeds, they were not crossbred with cats in the wild. They were tame, extremely affectionate, and mellow, known for their ability to sleep for hours in their owner's lap.

The grand champion Bombay on the cover was from a cattery in Gaithersburg, Maryland—just an hour north of where I lived—and the article included an interview with the breeder and her phone number. When I called to schedule a visit, Rosemary, the breeder, said her roommate used to commute to my neighborhood daily.

The drive to Rosemary's house took me through a rural area that reminded me of Wisconsin. A dozen vultures soared over fields and woods with their two-toned black wings opened into shallow V signs, their bodies rocking in midair. Starlings flocked in the low sky, forming blurry connect-the-dot pictures between power lines. My destination was a cul-de-sac in a subdivision with a row of nearly identical brown bungalows, and Rosemary's house had a wheelchair ramp leading up to the front door; unopened bags of cat litter and cardboard boxes of cat food lined almost the entire incline. A woman in her seventies came to the door in a navy-blue sweatshirt and baggy jeans, her hair cut short and permed to give it body, the way American mothers styled their hair in the 1980s.

I followed her into the living room, which was dark even on a sunny September afternoon because the ceiling was low and a high-backed couch blocked the windows. The room had two armchairs, a rocking chair, another couch against the opposite wall, and a desk in the corner. A dozen piles of fabric scraps and magazines and more boxes of cat food sat on the floor. Wandering around this obstacle course were six compact-looking cats, five dark brown and one pure black, all with the round faces of cherubs and the copper-yellow eyes of the devil.

I sat down on the couch by the windows, from which I could see down a long narrow hallway blocked off by a baby gate.

"I know I was in *Cat Fancy* for their Bombay Cat breed profile," Rosemary explained as the six cats came up to sniff my hand, "but I mostly raise Burmese."

Burmese cats had been featured in another issue of the magazine. The first Burmese in America in the early twentieth century had been a cross between a brown cat from Burma and a Siamese. The resulting kittens were known to be intelligent and affectionate like the Siamese but calmer and quieter. The Bombay in turn was bred from the American Shorthair and the Burmese. I was surrounded by Miles's distant cousins, all of them genetically predisposed to be like him, though not completely.

Over the next hour, Rosemary told me about the numerous award-winning cats she had raised. Every few minutes, she'd get up from her armchair and flip through the piles of magazines on the floor, their pages stuffed with photographs and certificates. She pulled out manila folders from her desk drawers and more photographs of her grand champions—glossy and wallet-sized, like the kind in high school yearbooks. I half-expected signatures and fond messages scrawled on the back from Harvest, Pumpkin, Bailey, Maple, or Midnight. I couldn't tell the cats apart or keep them straight in my head.

Every other breeder I knew had simple, straightforward systems for reserving a kitten. You wrote a check for a nonrefundable deposit and then you were put on a waiting list. The breeder would call you when a kitten was available. Rosemary

would only accept a deposit after the kittens were old enough—
about eight weeks—to get their first vaccination. Potential clients
had to telephone her for the exact date and then mail, FedEx, or
personally deliver their checks from that day on. Kittens were
chosen in the order their checks were received. She made it sound
like a mob of people would be knocking down her door on the
appointed day to hand-deliver their deposits.

The six cats roaming around her living room comprised her
entire roster of breeding females or "queens." All of them were
expecting kittens in about a month. You didn't have to be a math
whiz to figure out that there would be at most four or five Bombay
kittens from the one black cat and five times as many from the
chocolate brown cats, one of whom—Zena—had deposited a
couple of fur balls, a toy mouse, and felt fish at my feet.

When I reached down to pick up one of the toys, Zena
pressed her cheek against my fingers and purred. Her wide face
and slightly bulging eyes looked at once sweet and sagacious. She
was eager to play but not pushy. Of the six cats, including the
Bombay, she clearly had the best personality.

"I changed my mind," I told Rosemary. "I'd rather have one of
the Burmese kittens. I'll be in touch when the time approaches."

I held up the fur ball for Zena to see before I tossed it. She
dashed across the room, put it in her mouth, and brought it back.
Then she sat down next to me and waited patiently, her eyes on
my hand as I reached for the second fur ball. As soon as I tossed
it, she trotted across the room, picked it up, returned to my side,
and dropped it at my feet.

I played fetch with Zena for a few more minutes, then got up
from the couch and maneuvered my way around the wheelchair
to the front door, down the ramp lined with supplies, to my car.
Rosemary's bungalow was the opposite of the house on the hill

Cat and Bird

where Miles was born. Her six breeding queens roamed around the small living room, almost forming a pack, though cats are not known to do so. Inside the magazines on the floor, pictures of her prizewinning felines mingled with glamour shots of the purebreds from around the world. The house Miles grew up in was full of partitions, with each cat staying where it belonged. Already, the two cats had a story together, of opposites coming together to live in harmony.

I called Rosemary every week to ask when the kittens would be born and when they were getting their first vaccination so I could be the first to arrive at her house with a check and choose my kitten. I didn't mind if I came across as a lunatic; even Gail thought I was nuts when we went to a concert of church music—our neighbor, the violinist, was singing in the choir—and when there came a hymn about waiting for the Christ Child to be born, I leaned over and whispered, "I get it now. I'm waiting for the messiah."

My feline Burmese messiah already had a name: Jackson, after Jackson Browne, the singer whose last name matched the color of the kitten's fur. While considering the Bombay as a companion for Miles, I had researched the names of famous Black Panthers. Most of the Panthers, I was dismayed to discover, had led violent and tragic lives. Jackson Browne, however, was still playing music and looking as handsome as ever. I had missed his concert in Osaka when I was seventeen because I was stupid enough to tell my stepmother where my friends and I were going. But soon I'd be able to spend every evening with his namesake, a feline rock star. The "real" Miles Davis and Jackson Browne had never appeared at the same music festival—neither played at Woodstock or Live Aid 1985—but our life together would be a story set in an alternative universe.

Finally, the day came when Rosemary was accepting deposits, so I drove to her house with Gail to deliver the check and choose my kitten. At two o'clock, we were the only ones there. The dozen male Burmese kittens had been placed in a round, fleece-lined cat bed, each wearing a different colored hair band around his neck. I picked them up, one by one, as though sampling hors d'oeuvres. They all tolerated being turned over, dangled upside-down, touched all over, and kissed on the head and the belly. Gail's job was to distract Rosemary while I did this battery of docility tests so Rosemary wouldn't notice me manhandling her kittens. The kitten with the green hair band started purring the moment I picked him up.

"This one," I told Rosemary, "with the green band. This is Jackson, my cat."

Rosemary checked her chart and said, "That's one of Zena's."

Jackson needed two more shots and a course of deworming pills before Rosemary would release him in mid-January. I visited him every week, worrying that something would happen to him before I could take him home. Rosemary was preparing for Christmas. At each visit, there were larger piles of fabric scraps from which she was sewing cat and baby blankets, indistinguishable even by size. She also had scissors, wrapping paper, ribbons, string, tape, tags, and more magazines and boxes of supplies scattered all over the living room where the two dozen kittens and six queens were running around. I had always sequestered my cats in another room before I brought out ribbons or strings they could swallow by mistake. A friend's cat once ate a piece of yarn and it got tangled around his intestine. The cat was okay, after $4,000 of tests, surgery, and hospital stays for him and many sleepless nights for the human. Rosemary's house looked booby-trapped with every possible danger a kitten could face. The dark brown carpet in the living room was the same color as Jackson's fur. I didn't understand how any of the kittens escaped being stepped on or crushed under the rocking chair or smashed between the screen door and the front door.

I stayed about an hour, long enough to play with Jackson, hold him and carry him around, and hear another installment of the story of Rosemary's life, which included having been married to a Vietnam veteran who decided "he'd rather be a pothead than a father" and raising her son alone. He now lived in a nearby town with his wife and children. She mentioned working as a middle school social studies teacher before her retirement. Mostly, though, she talked about the cat shows she was preparing to attend and updated me every week about which kittens got promised to their new owners.

On one afternoon visit, I followed Jackson down the hallway. The baby gate had been removed, and I found myself in a dining room with a queen-sized bed shoved against the dish cabinet. A woman with long gray hair was sitting propped up on pillows, wearing a pink flannel nightgown and watching TV with a headset.

"Hi," I said, grabbing Jackson and holding him up for her to see, as though he was evidence of my harmlessness. "I'm here to visit my cat."

"I'm Pat, Rosemary's roommate," the woman said, taking off the headset momentarily and then putting it back on before I could speak.

"Nice to meet you," I said before beating my retreat to the living room, where Rosemary was wrapping Christmas presents for her grandchildren. I set Jackson on the floor and picked up one of the dozen feathered wands lying around. Immediately, he reared up on his hind legs like a miniature bear. Rosemary talked about her grandchildren, and then she said she was running out of time to prepare for Christmas because she had to spend the next few days driving her roommate to clinics. It was the first time she mentioned her roommate since our phone conversation, but she didn't explain their relationship or the nature of Pat's physical ailment. She didn't even say the obvious, such as, "By the way, that was my roommate you just met."

For all the time we spent together and the stories she told me, it occurred to me there was so much I didn't know about her.

Come January, twelve-week-old Jackson trotted out of the living room to meet me in the foyer. I scooped him up and put him inside the carrier I'd brought. I handed Rosemary the check for the second half of my payment, she held the door open for me, and I carried Jackson down the wheelchair ramp. All the way to the car, I could hear him purring inside the bag. When we got home and I set him loose, he walked around as though he had never lived anywhere else. Miles had no choice but to accept him. He tried to act aloof for a day—looking askance at Jackson and refusing to purr for me—but soon, the two of them were sitting side by side as Ernest and Miles had done.

Two days later, when I took Jackson to the animal hospital for his initial check-up, the nickel-sized bald spot on his head turned out to be ringworm, a highly contagious fungal infection among humans as well as animals. I had noticed the spot right away when we got home from Rosemary's house and I could see him for the first time in natural light. Ringworm wasn't a life-threatening condition. If it had been discovered earlier, however,

Cat and Bird

I wouldn't have been able to take him home since no breeder would knowingly sell a kitten with a health problem.

The veterinarian said I could keep Jackson and Miles apart for sixteen weeks—the length of a semester—or treat them both. Even if there had been space in my apartment, I wouldn't have quarantined Jackson. The cats were getting along so well. I didn't want to separate them and run the risk of ruining their relationship.

"You got out of there just in time," I told Jackson on our way home.

The joint reign of Miles and Jackson began with twice weekly baths and daily pills.

I had been brushing Miles's teeth every night since he came to live with me six months earlier, so opening his mouth and cramming a pill down his throat was only a minor adjustment. He ran when he sensed that the toothpaste and the pill were in the offing but relaxed as soon as I caught him.

Jackson was the mellowest, most confident cat I'd ever met. Glossy brown like a little duke dressed in a mink coat, he would claw his way up my legs and onto my lap whenever he wanted attention and press his whole body hard against my hand till I started petting him. The pill regimen didn't faze him a bit.

For the baths, I carried both cats into the bathroom and shut the door. It seemed prudent to start with Miles, the older and more cautious one.

Wet the fur thoroughly, the directions said on the medicated shampoo bottle. *Apply and lather, being careful to avoid the eyes and the mouth. Leave on for ten minutes and rinse.*

I dunked Miles in a dishpan full of warm water, doused him with the shampoo I'd shaken to a full "lather" inside a plastic bottle made for squirting barbecue sauce on spareribs or chicken wings, then wrapped him in a towel and held him in my lap for ten minutes. He only started squirming and meowing about eight minutes in. By the time he was being dunked again for the rinse, he was yowling, but he never bit or scratched me. I towel-dried him, put him on the bath mat, and repeated the process with Jackson, who was so small that he resembled a hamster when wet. The cats scampered out when I opened the door, but within ten minutes, they came up to me, purring. I petted their still-damp fur and told them that the whole ordeal was a team-building exercise. Unlike the pills, which had to be given for sixteen weeks, the baths could stop after six weeks if Jackson had three consecutive "negative" readings on his skin test. Miles and I never developed ringworm, though only Miles received preventive treatment. Humans don't need special shampoos and pills, my doctor assured me, because if we get infected, we can use external medication without having to wear a cone-shaped collar to keep ourselves from licking it off.

I called Rosemary and made it clear that I wasn't interested in bringing Jackson back. I wasn't asking her to give me my money back or pay for the treatments.

"The vet said I should let you know because ringworm is contagious. It would be almost impossible for some of your other cats not to have it too."

"I don't know where that came from," Rosemary said. "I've never had a problem with that." She wouldn't even say the word "ringworm."

"I don't think Jackson caught ringworm on his way home in the car."

Rosemary stonewalled me, so I gave up.

Ringworm spreads through microscopic spoors that can lie dormant for months. Getting rid of it requires not only medicating and bathing the cats but also washing the sheets and towels that came into contact with their skin and fur and cleaning the house regularly. As I ran down to the laundry room with loads of wash every day, I began to feel sorry for Rosemary. Not all cats exposed to the spoors develop symptoms right away, so when we talked on the phone, she could have really believed that the cats at her cattery were uninfected. Sooner or later, however, bald spots would start showing up. If I'd called her again and offered to help clean the house and bathe the cats, she might have told me the truth.

But now that my home felt complete again with two kittens chasing each other and climbing onto my lap to sleep, exhausted, with their paws tangled together, I didn't like to leave except to run, teach, and shop for groceries. So I decided that Rosemary—and the other people who had gotten kittens from her—would surely receive help from their friends and veterinarians. My friends asked to see the new kitten even after I told them about the ringworm. So I hosted dinner parties for them, a reception for the dozen people who were attending a writers' conference in the neighborhood, and a "kitten shower" for Jackson (guests donated money to the Humane Society in his name). No one caught ringworm, perhaps because of the rolls of paper towel and liquid soap I provided for frequent handwashing. Soon, Rosemary's bungalow seemed like a place in another galaxy.

Every time Jackson clambered onto my lap, demanding to be petted, I thought that growing up in Rosemary's house had served him well after all. Nothing scared or surprised him. He was extremely assertive: instead of meowing and complaining, he muscled his way into my arms whenever he wanted attention. The weekly skin test at the hospital was a simple swab on the bald spot where his hair soon grew back, and he purred throughout the procedure. It was almost as though we were paying social calls to visit the adoring staff. I couldn't believe how easy it was to be in the hospital with a pet who only had a minor problem.

For their semiweekly baths, Miles sat wrapped in his blue towel like someone enduring a beauty treatment; Jackson's eyes looked even bigger when the rest of his body was drenched. They made me laugh in the same room where, earlier in the year, I had held Ernest and Algernon wrapped in their towels for their hydration treatments. I'd felt calm and competent with Ernest and Algernon—being able to help them, even temporarily, was a consolation—but now, the twice-a-week shampooing was a comedy routine. I almost missed it when we didn't have to do it anymore, but then Jackson found other ways to make me laugh. Aside from turning out to be just what I'd wished for—sweet, confident, and relaxed—he had a talent for slapstick. He spun around batting at his own tail, lay down on the floor with a thud no Siamese cat would make, and often misjudged my height while trying to jump onto my shoulder and ended up sliding down my back. He was a great contrast to Miles, who could sneak up behind me and silently jump on my shoulder, always landing securely on his soft paws. Miles could have trained as a ninja. Jackson—if he was a criminal—would have gotten a parking ticket while waiting in the getaway car during a bank heist.

After the ringworm went away, the chocolate brown fur on Jackson's head felt so smooth and plush that "Plush-Head" became one of his many nicknames. When he turned three, Jackson sent Rosemary a card, along with a few pictures of himself sleeping and playing with Miles: *Dear Rosemary, I am doing very well and hope you are too. Love, Jackson.*

Jackson and I didn't hear back from her, but I hope she is keeping the pictures between the pages of her *Cat Fancy*, giving Jackson and Miles places of honor among the grand champions of the feline universe.

Chapter Thirteen

Cat Tricks

Miles and Jackson let me hold them aloft and do bird imitations to amuse our guests: a chimney swift circling the chimney and diving in, a turkey vulture swaying in the air current, and a nuthatch walking headfirst down a tree trunk. I dangled each cat upside down like a bat, then I put him on my head like a hat. Or I held him upright and walked him across the room on his hind legs, a bipedal cat, and then grabbed his hind legs, tipped him over, and pushed him forward on his front legs like a wheelbarrow.

"I can't believe they let you do all that," said Susan, who described her own cat, Henry, as "full of vinegar." A tabby rescued directly off the street, Henry liked to roll around on the floor, looking adorable, only to trick you into petting him so he could sink his teeth into your hand.

Miles and Jackson were bred and raised to be docile and affectionate. As a finale to our show, I'd pick up each cat and pretend to eat him: first like corn on the cob, then like a burrito, and finally like a chocolate bunny. My favorite thing to do with them, alone or in front of company, was to pick them up and bury my face in their stomachs, which were soft and warm, like bread right out of the oven.

"It's the price of living here," Susan told my cats, "You had to give up your dignity."

What Miles and Jackson really had to give up, though they didn't know it, was the freedom to roam and hunt. To compensate, I installed bird feeders and potted plants on the window ledge, scattered toys throughout the apartment, and had

Cat and Bird

a set of special shelves built into the living room wall to serve as cat perches. Every day, the three of us run around with toy birds and mice on strings, and Miles loves to fetch his orange chew toy. If I'm busy, he plays with the toy on his own, tossing it up into the air with his mouth and batting it down with his paw, then securing it to the floor as he tries to rip it apart with his teeth and claws. If a mouse ever came into our apartment, this is precisely how Miles would dispatch it. Jackson goes crazy over feather toys. He watches the birds outside the window with a hunter's interest and occasionally swats at the flocks of doves.

House cats are obligate carnivores born to hunt. When a group of indoor-outdoor cats were outfitted with GPS devices or miniature cameras ("cat-cams") on their collars to track their movements, their owners were shocked to see the dangerous places they would visit regularly, such as construction sites and storm sewers, not to mention the frequency of their skirmishes with other cats and predators, and the number of birds and small mammals they killed. The owners believed it was cruel to prevent cats from following their natural instincts. Few were convinced that their pets should remain indoors, even after seeing the entire cat-cam footage and learning that the average life expectancy of a cat who roams outdoors is four to five years, no longer than the lifespan of a songbird. To most, their freedom was precisely their appeal: cats went to places we could not follow them, did things wild and risky, and came back to us like kites that had soared above the power lines but returned in one piece.

I understand the appeal of daily encounters with an animal whose life remains a mystery. Every spring, I watch for the return of ruby-throated hummingbirds. The first migrants, both males and females, arrive at my window in early May, but their appearance is sporadic because they are just moving through the area. Once settled into their breeding territory, hummingbirds are extremely territorial and make rounds of their preferred feeding sites in the same sequence throughout the day, so in June and July, when just one female comes around the clock to my feeder, I assume it's an individual nesting nearby. Her last appearance is always at dusk: she samples the flowers first and then the sugar-water feeder, dipping in and out to take several long drinks.

Every night around eight thirty, I sit at my table with a cup of coffee and wait for her. If the cats are awake, I hold them tight on my lap so they won't scare her and cause her to disappear into the murky gray air without taking her fill. In the hours between dusk and dawn, if she hasn't eaten enough or the night is unseasonably cold, she will have to slow down her heartbeat from 250 beats a minute to as low as fifty beats and enter a state of torpor to conserve her body's energy reserves. Her temperature may drop from 110°F to 55°F, and there is no guarantee that she will wake up and be at my feeder in the morning. Ours is a one-sided relationship. The hummingbird isn't coming to have a drink with me; she doesn't even know I'm there. Still, this nightly visitation feels like a miracle and an honor, an encounter with a spirit who is at once fragile and tenacious.

Female hummingbirds tend their nests alone without the male's help, and they will defend their young by dive-bombing large predators, including roaming cats, but once the young are able to fly, the family disperses immediately. Unlike the sparrows that feed their fledglings beak to beak on the window ledge, hummingbirds never return to the feeder with their children in tow. Each hummingbird migrates without its own kind, in a mixed flock consisting of other bird species. Ornithologists have yet to understand how a first-year hummingbird can find its way across the Gulf of Mexico to a wintering ground it has never seen.

My cats are descended from another solitary species, but they are the opposite of wild or mysterious. Letting them roam across our backyard will do nothing to restore the natural order. House cats are infamous for slowly killing every small creature they can hook with their paw, tear into with their teeth, maim and let go, only to catch again. They are also infamous for not eating all, or even much, of what they kill. That is their nature, they can't help it. But what happens to the birds, small mammals, lizards, and insects who cross their path isn't natural. Like any invasive species, house cats who roam outdoors harm the ecological balance of their environment. It's one of the reasons I keep my cats inside. The other reason, of course, is that a cat who goes outdoors becomes a part of the food chain: there are animals—invasive or otherwise—who can devour them.

After ten thousand years of domestication, house cats—even feral cats who have never spent a day inside anyone's house—are more predictable than mysterious. I know more about my cats than I do about any human being. Due to the guilty choice I made to acquire them from breeders instead of a shelter, I even saw where they were born and how they were raised. In the 660-square-foot space where they came to live with me, not much ever happens that I don't witness firsthand. My cats don't connect me to the thrills and dangers of the great outdoors. They anchor me to the safety and comfort of home. The best thing I can do for them is to protect them from the natural world—and to protect the natural world from them.

Miles and Jackson are not the only cats to live happily indoors with the human companion they love. All pet owners are occasionally criticized for doting on our pets, but the worst contempt is reserved for women with cats, the proverbial cat ladies whose homes are overrun by felines that are only taking advantage of them. People who hate cats—ailurophobes—fixate on the notion that cats control us rather than allowing us to control them. They believe dogs are loyal and cats are aloof, selfish, and incapable of loving us. In reality, with any pet, the ideal relationship is a friendly give-and-take of mutual love and understanding, with humans in charge of the ground rules and long-range plans.

I learned about clicker training at a cat show, where a dozen cats appeared on the stage to sit, shake hands, stand up on their hind legs, and jump through hoops. Every cat looked poised and confident. Dogs routinely fetch sticks and catch Frisbees. At state fairs in the Midwest, I'd seen pigs race around tracks and llamas (led by their handlers) navigate obstacle courses. But all these other animals paled in comparison. Only a cat could exude such self-possession while performing tricks for food. The trainers were using dried chicken liver treats and thumb-sized plastic devices that made a sharp clicking noise when pressed. They said anyone could teach cats of any age a repertoire of tricks.

Clicker training is a form of operant conditioning that uses positive reinforcement, usually a food treat, and a noise from a clicker to mark the behavior. The training method, developed in the 1940s by two of B. F. Skinner's students, who taught pigeons to push balls with their beaks, became popular in the 1990s when Karen Pryor, an American biologist and animal behavior psychologist, started giving seminars to dog owners. Now it's used for horses, cats, birds, and rabbits, as well as dogs. In spite of its origins in behavior modification, the current practice emphasizes exercise and enrichment.

The first step involves teaching your pet that the sharp noise from the clicker means he will get a treat. Once the pet understands this basic concept, you can teach him that he has to do something—such as raising one paw for a handshake—to cause a "click and treat." I used dehydrated shrimp, recommended by my veterinarian, who had taught one of her cats to turn her bedside lamp on and off.

I worked with one cat at a time while the other waited his turn shut up in the bathroom: Miles first, then Jackson. It took each cat less than a minute to understand the basic concept of "click and treat." Associating noise and food comes naturally to cats, who use their hearing (as well as sight and smell) to locate prey, and the dehydrated shrimp was a big draw.

Cats also instinctively touch things with their nose. For the first command, "Touch," I held a pencil in front of my cat's nose so he couldn't miss; I clicked and treated when the tip of his nose touched the tip of the pencil. This too only took a minute for them to understand. Before the end of the first session, each cat was following the pencil around and standing on his hind legs to touch his nose to it. Now the pencil had become a useful tool. For the next lesson, "Sit," I held the pencil slightly above my cat's head so he would, naturally, look up and begin to sit. The instant his butt touched the floor, I clicked and treated. Miles and Jackson learned "Sit" in one session and "Come Here" in another (I pointed first with the pencil and then just with my finger).

I never doubted that my cats would catch on if I was consistent with my part of the exercise. Still, I was thrilled by how quickly they mastered the basics. Of course, they had been learning to read me long before the clicker entered our lives.

Ever since they were kittens, Miles and Jackson had recognized the sound of my footsteps and the patterns of my activity: they correctly anticipated when I was coming home, going to bed, or preparing for the cleaning lady's biweekly visits and would greet me at the door, hop on the bed, or hide under it accordingly. Just like I knew everything about them, they knew everything about me, at least within the territory we shared. They'd been practicing for years to interpret the cues I had given them at random; now I was learning how to direct their attention deliberately.

Every advanced trick we worked on was built on the basics from the first few sessions. I taught Jackson to stand on his hind legs like a bear by holding the pencil high above his head. Miles is one of those cats that habitually uses his long front leg like an arm, so I trained him to sit and raise one paw to high-five me. I held the pencil across my palm for him to touch his paw to it, and when he did it consistently, I could omit the pencil and get him to tap my palm. The secret was to start with something that came naturally to them and not to keep pushing when they didn't understand what they were supposed to do. In teaching Jackson to shake hands, I got confused about which hand or paw was right or left, so he raises his left paw now instead of his right. I decided that was okay; the feline handshake didn't have to duplicate the human version exactly.

To teach the cats to jump over a stick ("Pony"), I first put the stick on the floor and led them over it with the pencil. They were clicked and treated every time they walked over it. Once they could consistently do that, I raised it a little higher each time until they had to jump. Soon, all I had to do was hold up the stick and they just jumped over it. By the time I found the right hoop—it was actually a Hula-Hoop for a child—Miles and Jackson were both experts at "Pony." The hoop ("Dolphin") then slightly modified the earlier trick. I also realized, somewhere in the process of all these jumps, that the cats could learn from each other if I trained them together. Miles figured out both Pony and Dolphin first, and then Jackson imitated him.

I coached Miles to stand on the edge of the table, leap up through the hoop, and land gracefully on the floor. With his long pale body and masked face—like blue-gray suede—he looked fantastically aerodynamic. This advanced version of Dolphin is the showiest trick in our repertoire, but Jackson—whose leaps are not as spectacular due to his chubby legs—also had his moments to shine. He could launch himself straight up from the floor in a vertical jump, all four feet in the air and his body slightly bent at the waist, to bat at the feathers I dangled above his head. Thanks to his huskier figure and lower center of gravity, he could hold his "Bear" pose (standing on his hind legs) in perfect form and even extend his hind legs completely and stretch his front legs over his head ("Grizzly"). Taller and wobblier, Miles wasn't as comfortable on his hind legs.

Jackson is the first and only cat of mine to try and dash out our door into the building's hallway. So instead of picking him up and forcibly removing him from the doorway, I taught him to go up on the stool I'd placed next to the door and sit. Once he was seated, I said, "Stay." Then I counted to three, tapped the floor, and said "Here," and when he jumped off the stool for that spot, I clicked, tossed the treat for him to eat on the floor, and opened the door while he was busy eating. After he learned this sequence, I opened the door while Jackson was seated on the stool and asked him to "Stay, Stay, Stay" until I closed it. I could walk out into the hallway, with him on the stool, looking at me through the open door. He only jumped off the stool when I came back and closed the door behind me. Then I made him sit and shake hands before I clicked and gave him a treat. This sequence is the hardest trick for him, though, especially if we're in a real-life situation in which the door is open because I'm carrying my groceries, pulling my bike into the foyer, or having guests come and go.

We live on the third floor, and the doors to the stairway are always closed, so it's not as though Jackson, if he did slip out, could go anywhere. Gail and Beth, who live on my floor, let their cats run in the hallway for exercise. But I feel slighted when Jackson dashes out, as if he wants to run away from home, even though I know it's just an expression of his curious and outgoing nature. He's also the only cat ever to try and push his way into every closet or cupboard door I open. He simply loves to investigate. I've trained Miles to stay by the door and high-five me, giving him something to do while Jackson does his "Stay" trick, but Miles never runs out no matter how long the door is open. His lifelong project, I'm sure, is to train me to stay indoors. He also sees no point in going into closets and cupboards— spaces I reach into but never enter. In fact, he gets anxious when the two of us are not on the same side of the door.

Miles loves to sprint from room to room inside our apartment, and "Sit, Sit, Sit" in all the places I point to with my finger. Like me, he is a runner. If he were on the track team, he could run the mile, half-mile, and one thousand meters—my events in high school—while Jackson, who has the physique and swagger of a shot-putter, would dedicate himself to the field events that I failed to master. Jackson would never send the shot straight up in the air and have to duck out of its way or, like me, release the discus half a turn too soon and watch helplessly as it sailed toward the stands (thank God they were empty). He was already a champion vertical jumper.

Cat and Bird

Miles, who was curious and eager to meet visitors when he was a kitten, grew up to be shy with everyone but me. At two years old, he started hiding in the bedroom when we had more than three or four people in the living room. He would emerge toward the end of the party and run around meowing. "Go away, go away," he was screaming; it was midnight, and he'd had enough. During smaller dinner parties, he stayed in the living room and draped himself across my lap in such a way that he could pointedly stare at my friends. Whenever I stood up to get more food or drinks, he'd follow me into the kitchen, refusing to be left alone with those people.

Jackson, on the other hand, remained gregarious and nonchalant, always happy to be picked up and carried around by anyone. In effect, Jackson had made way for Miles to be who he had wanted to be all along, a one-person cat who doesn't like strangers or new situations. And yet, in spite of his shyness, once he learned some tricks, Miles could be lured to perform. He overshadowed Jackson with his spectacular leaps through the Hula-Hoop and his unmistakable self-satisfied expression when he perched on the cat tree and raised his paw for a high-five. "He's so beautiful," people would sigh as he dashed back to the bedroom. It reminded me of the evenings I came out of my room to play the piano for my mother's guests, only to run away at the sound of a compliment.

The goal of clicker training is not to control your cats but to figure out, together, how to choreograph a sequence of cues and gestures that result in the mutually satisfying click of success. The whole process must have seemed to my cats as if they were teaching me how to produce the treat.

Our training success was proof that cats are no more aloof or indifferent than other animals who are regularly trained by the same method. However, their learning styles are different. Presented with multiple levers or buttons in scientific studies, dogs, monkeys, and pigeons all persisted through the trial-and-error process until they figured out which lever or button caused the treats to fall down the chute. Cats learned only if they happened to press the right lever early in the session. Otherwise, after pressing the wrong levers and getting no treats, they lost interest and walked away. Like the classic underachievers among us, cats become discouraged when a task challenges them too much. But that doesn't mean they are lazy and selfish. While dogs, monkeys, and pigeons are omnivores who must look for food in a variety of settings, cats have evolved to hunt prey whose patterns of behavior are highly predictable. To persevere through repeated failures, to keep waiting for food in a place where they have had no success, is not in their nature.

It isn't in mine, either. My report cards before the last two years of college were filled with As and Ds and not much in between. In track, I gave up on field events and concentrated on running, the activity I felt I was born for. My learning style is feline: I learn only if I'm doing well and having fun. So it made perfect sense to me to start Miles and Jackson on easy tricks, and when they couldn't figure out what they were supposed to do, I was happy to back off before they got bored and frustrated. Even though taking up clicker training was my idea, the actual process required a give-and-take that all three of us enjoyed. That was the whole point of the exercise.

Every night before bed, my cats and I review our clicker repertoire to remember our accomplishments and end the day on a positive note. We move from room to room, performing a

Cat and Bird

ten-minute sequence of the skills we've mastered: Sit, Bear, Stay, Come, Sit, Pony, Sit, Shake Hands, Sit, High-Five, Sit. Miles's dolphin dive is the nightly finale. After drawing circles around me for hours, he ends his day by launching himself into the circle I hold in the air. He jumps because he can trust me.

Chapter Fourteen

My Pillow Book

On my summer runs in Washington, DC, the warm air steeped through the thick foliage overhead reminded me of Kyoto, where the tenth-century writer Sei Shōnagon had served as a lady-in-waiting to the empress and recorded her impressions of court life in *The Pillow Book*. Shōnagon's imperial garden would have been immersed in the same liquid light, which made her relish the nightfall all the more.

"In summer the nights," she wrote. "Not only when the moon shines, but on dark nights too, as the fireflies flit to and fro, and even when it rains, how beautiful it is." She could have been describing the fireflies flickering over the azaleas and Japanese laurels on our grounds and the frequent pop-up thunderstorms that drenched the bamboo groves out back.

When the first hummingbird appeared at my window while I was watering the red petunias like the ones in my childhood garden, I believed I was receiving a visitation from an entity that was half my mother and half Shōnagon. Both women loved flowers, birds, and clothes, equally drawn to nature and artifice. Shōnagon, who included "sparrows feeding their young" on her list of "Things That Make One's Heart Beat Faster," never encountered a hummingbird. But if she had seen the one at my window, she would have pronounced her "resplendent," like the imperial retinue in their ceremonial attire. Although the female hummingbird lacks the ruby gorget of her male counterpart, her iridescent green back resembles a jacket worn open over her white chest and belly. When she beats her wings faster to float up over the flowers, a line of white appears on the tips of her dark green tail feathers, like the crisp hem of an undergarment intentionally revealed. Court ladies of Shōnagon's day wore twelve layers of silk to produce a similar effect.

Little is known about Shōnagon except that she was born around 965 AD to the family of a provincial government official. She went to the capital in 993 to serve Empress Sadako and left the court in 1000 when Sadako died in childbirth. In one of her entries, Shōnagon claims that she wrote *The Pillow Book* for her own amusement to ponder "odd facts, stories from the past, and all sorts of other things, often including the most trivial material." But the book-in-progress was regularly circulated at the palace and read by the imperial couple, the courtiers, and the waiting ladies.

Sadako was the first wife of the emperor (he was twelve and she fourteen when they married in 990), but there were several rival wives and consorts, each backed by a political faction. Shōnagon, who wrote admiringly about the clever conversations between the empress and emperor (who mostly talked about poetry), never referred to the numerous political intrigues or even to the fact that after the death of her powerful father, Sadako lost the emperor's favor to her cousin Akiko. Neither did she comment on the famines, fires, and outbreaks of smallpox that anyone at court would have heard about. Aside from the stories she knew by heart through the literature and the oral tradition of her day, she wrote only about what she observed and experienced directly. Many of her entries are about human foibles.

Among the list of her "Hateful Things" are, "To envy others and complain about one's own lot; to speak badly about people; to be inquisitive about the most trivial matters and to resent and abuse people for not telling one, or, if one does manage to worm out some facts, to inform everyone in the most detailed fashion as if one had known all from the beginning." She would have hated the way we continue to jockey for status, using information in a never-ending game of one-upmanship.

Her mind was as nimble as a hummingbird: dipping into one flower, then the next, hovering in the air for a moment and then flying backward. She noticed the manners and conversations others took for granted and revealed the kind or cruel intention behind a small gesture, the hidden love or resentment that slipped out in a careless remark. When I moved to DC, I wondered what Shōnagon would have made of living a few miles from the National Mall in 2005. Surely, she would have noticed and been disgusted by the hypocrisy of her leaders. Even so, she might have only seen the White House on TV (which looked exactly the same, regardless of how close you lived to it), skimmed the daily news, donated money for others to defend human rights and global ecology, and gone back to composing a poem about a large mound of snow that eventually turned into a tiny ice sculpture. A thousand years later in the capital of my adopted country, I too wanted to focus on what I experienced and observed directly in my private life: birds and flowers at my window, conversations with my friends and neighbors, knitting, cooking, and eventually, cats. I could only hope that my "odd facts, stories from the past, and all sort of other things" might also illuminate some larger truths, however indirectly.

After Donald Trump's election in 2016, however, other writers who had never written about politics were attending rallies and posting their eyewitness accounts. It seemed inexcusable for any writer to avoid commenting directly on the backlash against feminism, the plight of asylum seekers at our borders, the numerous incidents of police brutality, and the continued environmental degradation of our whole planet. A memoirist whose work I admired signed up for a seminar to learn how to compose op-eds, though she reported, "I totally failed. Every op-ed I started turned into a personal essay." Never one to take a class in one of my weak subjects, I tried to teach myself by reading a selection of political commentary, articles, and op-eds every day, but I couldn't do it either.

I had never been able to write meaningfully about an event that was happening in real time. It took me a couple of years, usually more like a decade, to understand what I really thought about anything—especially anything upsetting—to make sure my reaction was more than a flash of anger or panic, and then, if I came up with a real insight, figure out how to use it to explore the painful or troublesome topic that had started me on the path. Though by then, things would have shifted, so an adjustment of focus was required. This nearly endless casting-about was exactly what I loved about writing, though. My mind could only move like a well-fed cat: circling its prey, napping to feign disinterest, and unable to resist a sidestep even, or especially, when the target was within reach. Overwhelmed by the enormity of the problem behind any current event, the microscopic vision I needed to analyze the facts, and the urgency to say something useful, I gave up and walked away like Dorian did from the mice he nibbled and left for me to finish. Most of the political writing I read depressed me. Even the books and articles I loved didn't inspire me to emulate them: in fact, they said the things I wanted to say so much better than I ever could, which led me to conclude that anything I came up with would be superfluous.

Perhaps Dorian brought those mice to me because he didn't know what to do with them and was hoping I could put them to better use. In spite of the hours he spent hunting every night, he didn't rid our house of mice—they only went away because Chuck and I eventually figured out where they were coming from and sealed the entries. Dorian's real specialty was keeping human visitors away. Likewise, the repertoire of tricks I could teach Miles and Jackson didn't include pointing to a spot away from me and asking them to lie down there, or putting food in front of them and telling them to wait to eat it until I said, "Okay." I could no more write political commentary or reportage than they could "Wait" or "Go Lie Down." A cat can only come to me and eat the food I offer without prevarication.

Except on a rare occasion when the blinds could be raised because no man was in the vicinity, Shōnagon observed the garden through the carefully angled slats of her windows. The multilayered clothes she wore, as well as the code of modesty, prevented her from going outside to wander the palace grounds, much less the capital of Kyoto itself. The empress and her ladies-in-waiting only left the palace on group excursions to view the cherry blossoms or the autumn leaves, hear the cuckoo's song, or attend religious festivals. They traveled in a caravan of ox-drawn carriages and saw most of the sights through the carriage windows.

In March 2020, the coronavirus pandemic held most of the world in lockdown, and suddenly, many of us were living like Shōnagon, who rarely saw outsiders face-to-face. Numerous courtiers came to the palace every day to deliver messages to the empress, but Shōnagon only spoke to them through the blinds that separated the interior corridor where she sat from the veranda that wrapped around the building. Any letter or gift they brought for the empress was slid under the blinds in a well-practiced no-contact delivery.

Cat and Bird

For Miles, the lockdown was a dream come true. I didn't go anywhere except to run, no one visited us, and nothing happened: a total cat day. This was exactly what he was longing for on those afternoons he paced around the foyer, meowing loudly while I put on my coat to drive to my teaching job twenty miles away.

"Don't worry," I used to remind him. "Tomorrow will be a total cat day again."

Now, with every day a total cat day, I could sit at my desk for as many hours as it took to finish my writing for the day or turn to my journal or read with the cats in my lap. The long quiet days with Miles and Jackson were peaceful, not lonely. Because we were all homebound, I talked to my out-of-town friends more regularly than I had in years, had coffee in the backyard with my neighbors, and organized socially distanced swift-viewing parties in the fall with a dozen lawn chairs set six feet apart in the driveway. It occurred to me that I was living the way my mother had when she was surrounded by her friends in the apartment complex or, for that matter, as Shōnagon had, confined to the palace with the empress and a dozen other ladies-in-waiting.

The nightly news about the infection rates and death tolls were devastating, but no one I knew got sick, so the pandemic seemed at once urgent and unreal. I thought about it the way I used to wake up every morning of my youth, heartbroken about my mother's suicide, anxious about my father's and stepmother's hostility, and fearful of our planet's destruction from nuclear bombs, only to spend the rest of my day fretting about making the starting lineup for the volleyball team. This time, too, the lesser worries were welcome distractions: the flour shortage, the restriction on toilet paper, the technological challenges of video-conferencing. And sheltering in place with my cats didn't feel like my life had changed that much.

Once school started online, Miles and Jackson acquired the one thing they'd been lacking: a public persona. They became stars of my Zoom classes, Jackson on my lap and Miles draped across the back of my neck or perched on the desk, displaying his profile to the screen. I couldn't resist putting Jackson on my head like a Davy Crockett hat or moving Miles across the screen in his flying posture ("Super Siamese"). At the end of each session, I held Jackson like a puppet and waved his paw to dismiss the class, a ritual that more than one student claimed was the highlight of their week. After a couple of online faculty meetings, colleagues I scarcely knew were talking about how beautiful, smart, and friendly my cats were. Other people's pets appeared on camera too, but mine wanted to perform. I quietly confided in a few friends, all of whom had pets of their own, that in spite of everything, the cats and I were having the best year of our lives together.

The one thing I missed was getting dressed up to go out. So I took comfort in what Shōnagon wrote in "Things That Make One's Heart Beat Faster": "To wash one's hair, make one's toilet, and put on scented robes; even if not a soul sees one, these preparations still produce an inner pleasure." Shōnagon understood that the pursuit of beauty was first and foremost for ourselves. She wouldn't have stayed all day in her pajamas or gone to the grocery store—the only place I went anymore—in sweaty running clothes just because no one saw, noticed, or cared about her attire. I also understood why my mother changed out of the shirt and slacks she wore around the house and put on a dress to go to the supermarket. Because she seldom left the house, each outing deserved careful planning. In the ten centuries between Shōnagon and Takako, not much had changed in how often or how far from home a respectable Japanese woman was allowed to roam. My mother had led a life of self-quarantine. On those weekends she took me to museums, dress shops, or public gardens, I was her caravan. With me seated across from her, she could occupy a table in a public place and have tea served to her in a pretty hand-painted cup.

For me, unlike for my mother, time alone was a welcome luxury. The lockdown reminded me of the month during my third-grade year when our school was closed to prevent the spread of chicken pox. I was the only child in the entire neighborhood who didn't get sick, so I rode my bike wherever I wanted, collected seashells on a deserted beach, and pretended I was building a city in an abandoned construction site by digging holes and stacking rocks into towers. When my friends recovered and could play again, I remembered the thrill of having the whole neighborhood to myself and felt almost sorry.

No one knows where Shōnagon went after the empress's death, though most ladies-in-waiting who retired from court joined Buddhist nunneries to live out their years in quiet contemplation. While she was writing *The Pillow Book,* however, Shōnagon had an active social life, receiving visitors through the bamboo screen during the day and spending the evening in the company of other women. Many of her anecdotes are about the games the empress and her ladies-in-waiting played nightly, usually featuring their ability to quote poetry or execute beautiful calligraphy. Shōnagon portrayed herself as a confident person who often had the right answer or a witty remark. She also admits, "If I am really close to someone, I realize that it would be hurting to speak badly about him and when the opportunity for gossip arises I hold my peace. In all other cases, however, I freely speak my mind and make everyone laugh." Far from shy or retiring, she might have been the life of the party, in the slightly frightening way that smart, opinionated people can be charismatic. But at the core of her observations, there is always a strong sense of independence.

In all of the 185 entries in *The Pillow Book*, Shōnagon doesn't mention one close friend, confidante, or mentor among the ladies-in-waiting she served with. The house they shared had the empress's chamber at its center, the only room with walls all around it. Surrounding this chamber on every side was an open corridor where the ladies-in-waiting slept, each one between a pair of painted folding screens used as room dividers. The only thing Shōnagon says about her family of origin was that she came from a long line of poets and scholars and hoped to honor them with her own knowledge of literature. There is no record of her ever being married or having children. It appears she spent her adulthood surrounded by other women but attached to no one. Still, she wrote that she pitied women who stayed at home with their husbands and children and wished they too could serve at the palace, so she must have found pleasure in sharing a home with her colleagues, even if none of them was her best friend. For her, as it was for my mother, communal living was surely more fulfilling than marriage.

Every night before going to sleep, alone in the small private space between the screens, Shōnagon would have pulled out her sheaf of paper—her "pillow book"—to record her impressions, lists, and stories. Although she didn't have her own cats, she observed those on the palace grounds. "I like a cat whose back is black and all the rest white," she writes. If she could see Miles and Jackson perched side by side on my desk, she would surely include them on her list of "Things that Make One's Heart Beat Faster."

Chapter Fifteen

Alone, Together

Birds kept falling in my path years after I left the Midwest. In Boston: two waxwing fledglings on a sidewalk, a cardinal nestling caught by a neighbor's cat, five house sparrows in a nest attached to a window air-conditioner that was about to be thrown away. I ferried them all to safety, knowing their lives would continue to be precarious. During my last winter there, on a morning after an ice storm, a starling flew down the chimney into my unused fireplace and left by the only window that was not frozen shut. I hoped the bird was a messenger from the past, sent to assure me that the cats and I would find another home, just as Dorian and I had after the first starling's visitation.

The summer I moved to Washington, DC, I came across a downy woodpecker fledgling huddled against the door of a restaurant a few blocks from my apartment. Fledglings often leave the nest before they are ready to fly and may need a few minutes to rest before they can take off on their own. The parents are usually nearby, ready to escort them to safety. So I stepped away to watch, but an elderly man who was walking by noticed too and approached the doorway. The bird began hopping across the sidewalk and into the street to get away from him. We were on a main thoroughfare, with cars coming and going. The fledgling disappeared under an SUV parked along the curb.

I asked the man to make sure no one got into the SUV while I crawled underneath it on my stomach. The bird was sitting next to one of the tires. I inched forward till I was almost an arm's length away. The only way to catch a frightened bird is just to grab him. I slid forward the final few inches and shot out my right hand. The fledgling peeped in protest when my fingers closed around his back. I crawled backward, careful not to lean on the hand with the bird in it, and pushed myself up onto the sidewalk.

My hand covered the bird's body, with my thumb and index finger circling his neck so only his head stuck out. Up close, I noticed a distinct pale red patch in the center of his crown, the mark of a juvenile. In all my years of birdwatching, I had never seen this detail so clearly. The pale red patch would fade over the summer; if he survived till spring, a brighter dot would appear on the back of his head. On a busy street full of human activity, a bird newly out of his nest had allowed me to hold him in my hand and observe his fleeting field mark. The fledgling opened and closed his beak several times, rotating his head in order to bite me. Someday, he would learn to drill holes in tree bark with his beak, but all he could do now was pinch the top of my thumb.

The street I was standing on—like the one in Kobe where I had placed the stunned sparrow in my tote bag—was lined with stores. Several people had gathered to watch. I assured them that I would deliver the bird to someone authorized to care for him. In a CVS store down the block, I found a sturdy paper bag on a rack of gift-wrapping supplies. The bird was peeping pretty loudly by the time I got to the counter to pay. I dropped him inside the bag and asked the astonished clerk for a stapler to seal the top and a pen to punch a few holes in the side. Out on the street, I flagged down a cab to drive us to the wildlife center across town, where the intake volunteer examined the fledgling and pronounced him to be in good condition. She would call one of the volunteers on her list. A month later, I received a postcard from the wildlife center informing me that the fledgling had been released in Rock Creek Park, not far from where I had found him.

Birds are regularly blamed for destroying crops, transmitting diseases, nesting in places where they're unwanted, and even for bringing down airplanes by colliding with them, but in truth, they save us more than we can ever save them. They protect us from insect infestations that would utterly destroy our health and our food supply. They pollinate flowers and disseminate seeds; the vegetation they protect, in turn, protects our land and our drinking water by preventing erosion. And like the proverbial canary in the coal mine, birds provide critical environmental data about toxins and other damaging elements. As in the folk stories my mother told me, birds reward our small kindnesses by shielding us from harm.

Their most important gift, however, is their mystery. No matter how carefully we observe their nesting habits and migration patterns, their lives largely occur in places we cannot reach. Even the common finches and sparrows that visit my window disappear into the trees at nightfall. The chimney swifts I held in my hands and launched back into the sky did not reveal if they were flying away from me for the first time or if the two of us had enacted this ritual of letting go the last time heavy rain poured down the chimney. We could have been walking up the basement steps into a summer morning again and again together for weeks, with only one of us aware of our association. Birds connect me, momentarily, to the boundless space only they can know.

In the woods in Wisconsin, I hiked for miles without seeing much of anything in order to stand in a secluded spot with my binoculars trained on the buffy eye-ring that distinguishes a Swainson's thrush from a gray-cheeked thrush. When the bird in my binoculars' vision matched the one whose field marks I had committed to memory, the world became seamless, with no difference between what was outside and inside my head. That moment of clarity was worth all the hours I spent meandering through the forest.

In writing, I find similar satisfactions in working, detail by detail, when a vague notion I have been entertaining for months, years, even decades, finally comes to me in the right form of expression, and I am surprised by a sentence, its instant familiarity, like a bird I've seen so many times in guidebooks suddenly materializing on a nearby branch. Then I can recognize the truth of it.

My favorite bird watching spot these days is my home, in the company of my cats. In the room where I write, my desk is about a foot away from a radiator that sits directly under the window. To keep the cats from climbing on the cast-iron pipes and getting burned, I had a shelf built to cover the radiator. Now, while I'm working, Miles and Jackson can safely perch on this shelf between the desk and the closed window and be only a few inches away from the steady stream of birds at the feeder outside. Either the birds don't see us or they understand something about the windowpane's impenetrability. They keep eating with their heads down, their beaks pounding the seeds with a staccato beat audible through the glass. I haven't seen so many wild birds up close every day since my years as a rehabilitator.

I marvel at the mixed flocks of tufted titmice, nuthatches, and chickadees, their movements like flickering lights, but Jackson's favorites are the mourning doves that swarm the feeder all day long. They are big and fat. They move slowly, and they sit in the same spot for minutes on end; they make a lot of noise when three or four of them arrive together. In

Shōnagon's world, they would be minor clerks in their gray and black jackets, visiting the imperial palace with petitions for advancement. Jackson watches them with his face pressed to the glass, his body like a torpedo ready to launch; his eyes, the color of gooseberries, register their every shift.

Miles lounges next to him, with his back to the window, his blue eyes on me. He falls asleep watching my fingers on the keyboard as Jackson crouches lower until he suddenly rears up on his hind legs and thumps the window with his front paw. Miles startles awake as the doves scatter, but he doesn't look back. Jackson studies the birds, ever hopeful he might catch one, while Miles could care less because he'd rather watch me.

The flocks of birds in the sky and in the trees are as elusive as the vague notions flitting in my mind's periphery. They approach the window in twos and threes, like ideas offering themselves for scrutiny. I wait for the right ones to land, at the precise moment when I am ready to see and understand them. My cats keep watch with me in our small private space between the screens. One looking out and one looking in, they are my lifelines: they draw me out and return me, restored, to myself.

My running route takes me past a strip mall that has a veterinary clinic. The parking lot is usually deserted in the early morning, but when I ran there during the pandemic, people would already be sitting in their cars or on benches that had been placed on the sidewalk, waiting for their pets. In order to protect the clinic's staff, humans were no longer allowed to go inside except for dire emergencies. When an appointment was over, a uniformed technician would bring out the dog on his leash or the cat in his carrier, and the two humans would stand six feet apart, talking through their masks. The veterinarian would call from inside the clinic to join the conversation. Morning after morning, I saw the same tableau: two people, a pet, a cell phone held between them with the vet's voice speaking. I sent silent good wishes to all of them, human and animal alike, as I sprinted past.

Three of my friends had to have their cats put to sleep in the pandemic's first months. They were allowed to be with their cats at the end, but for the weeks leading up to it, they could only discuss the prognosis and the treatment options with the veterinarians on the phone. Even though their cats were not young, losing them during an already difficult time was devastating. In November, when Miles suddenly stopped eating and threw up repeatedly, it was my turn to coordinate the appointments. They felt like covert operations requiring utmost precision and patience: a timed arrival and handover, numerous phone calls back and forth from inside the car, then the long wait to get him back. Finally, after four visits, the tests showed that Miles had Feline Inflammatory Bowel Disease, the same illness that had killed Ernest and Algernon at ten, Miles's exact age.

But Miles had a mild form of the disease, and it was in an early stage, so its progress could be slowed. The treatments had also improved vastly since Ernest's and Algernon's deaths. As soon as he got on his medication and his special prescription diet, Miles stopped throwing up and regained the weight he'd lost. Once again, he could jump from the floor to my shoulder, or leap through the Hula-Hoop and high-five me to receive the special prescription treats that were now available. After a year, I was able to taper off the medication and keep him healthy with just the restricted diet. The same veterinarian who had taken care of Ernest and Algernon—she cried when they died—has told me that if the special food keeps working, Miles could continue to thrive for years.

For Miles—and Jackson too—one-third of their allotted time still remains if they are destined for Dorian's lifespan. They may even outlive me if I turn out to be like my father, his sister, and their mother, all of whom died in their fifties and sixties from cancer. But I could just as easily live to be over ninety-five like my maternal grandmother and her two sisters, who were famous for their longevity. My cats and I may be at the same point on our journey, rounding the last bend of a long river, unable to see ahead but with reasons for optimism. I don't want to dwell on the fact that the one-third of life left to me is six times longer than theirs.

Each night, I sleep with Miles under the covers, the two us clinging to each other, his paws wrapped around my neck and his head tucked under my chin. Jackson curls up on my legs, serene and smooth as a stone in a Zen garden. With one cat to keep me afloat and the other to anchor me, I am where I belong, at home in the world.

Acknowledgments

This book began with an essay that appeared in *Conjunctions,* whose editor-in-chief, Bradford Morrow, has given me invaluable guidance over the years, always encouraging me to reach for the timeless over the timely. Robert Wilson at the *American Scholar* and Christina Thompson at *Harvard Review* helped me write two more essays that became the cornerstones for the book. Other parts of the book appeared, in different form, in the *Rumpus,* the *American Literary Review,* and *Wave Form: Twenty-First-Century Essays by Women. Cat and Bird* went through many more incarnations than the proverbial nine lives of felines; its continued survival was made possible only through the advice and support of Kathleen Anderson, my literary agent: thank you, Kathy, for your wisdom and persistence. I am grateful to Michael Jauchen, my editor at Belt Publishing, for asking all the right questions in the final push to make the book what it was always meant to be.

Many friends supported me through this and other writing projects. I'd like to thank Mako Yoshikawa for lifelong conversations about cats, clothes, and writing; James Neilson for sharing his belief in beauty; Timothy Denevi for being the best colleague and friend I could have asked for; Brighde Mullins for her generosity of spirit; and Henri Cole for being the touchstone of integrity in life as well as in writing. My gratitude to Jane Brox, who read an early version of the book and provided insights and encouragement, and to the rest of our Friday Zoom Group ("Cool Kids"): David Elliott, Hester Kaplan, Pamela Petro, and Sinan Ünel. At every place I taught, I was supported by friends whose work as writers and teachers inspired me: Courtney Brkic, Susan Shreve, Beverly Lowry,

Steven Goodwin, Allan Cheuse, Sally Keith, Deborah Kaplan, Tania James, Alexia Arthurs, Lan Samantha Chang, Suzanne Berne, Patricia Powell, and Alexandra Johnson.

Whenever I traveled, friends and neighbors cared for my cats in my absence—thank you, Beth Kaplan, Rachel and Justine Colson, Jen Packard, Rory Doehring, Gail Joice, Susan Bradfield, Stephen Ortado, Sue Thompson, and Molly O'Brien—or extended their hospitality to my cats when they accompanied me: thanks to Jerod Santek for hosting Oscar at the Loft and, two decades later, Miles at Write On, Door County; and Rob Sabal, who invited Miles and me to stay at his and Mako Yoshikawa's house when the hotel I reserved turned out not to accept cats ("Pet friendly only means dogs," said the clerk). A life with felines is at once stabilizing and turbulent. My gratitude to Chuck Brock for the thirteen years he lived with Dorian and me and for all the ensuing years through which he remained my friend.

About the Author

Kyoko Mori is the author of three nonfiction books (*The Dream of Water; Polite Lies; Yarn*) and four novels (*Shizuko's Daughter; One Bird; Stone Field, True Arrow; Barn Cat*). Her essays and stories have appeared in *The Best American Essays, Harvard Review*, the *American Scholar, Colorado Review, Conjunctions*, and others. She teaches in the MFA Program in Creative Writing at George Mason University and the Low-Residency MFA Program at Lesley University. Kyoko lives in Washington, DC, with her cats, Miles and Jackson.

9 781953 368690